Music and Magic

Music and Magic: Charlie Parker, Trickster Lives!

By

Frank A. Salamone

CAMBRIDGE SCHOLARS
PUBLISHING

Music and Magic: Charlie Parker, Trickster Lives!, by Frank A. Salamone

This book first published 2013

Cambridge Scholars Publishing

12 Back Chapman Street, Newcastle upon Tyne, NE6 2XX, UK

British Library Cataloguing in Publication Data
A catalogue record for this book is available from the British Library

Copyright © 2013 by Frank A. Salamone

All rights for this book reserved. No part of this book may be reproduced, stored in a retrieval system, or transmitted, in any form or by any means, electronic, mechanical, photocopying, recording or otherwise, without the prior permission of the copyright owner.

ISBN (10): 1-4438-5172-8, ISBN (13): 978-1-4438-5172-5

CONTENTS

Foreword vii
Marcus Aldredge

Acknowledgements xi

Introduction 1

Chapter One 5
Charlie Parker—Bird Lives!

Chapter Two 17
The Transformative Power of Jazz: Trickster and His Role in Jazz

Chapter Three 37
Jazz in Rochester in the Context of the Wider Scene

Chapter Four 51
Africa as a Metaphor of Authenticity

Chapter Five 67
The Culture of Jazz and Jazz as Critical Culture

Bibliography 89

Index 95

Foreword

Charlie Parker: Trickster Lives!

Frank Salamone's monograph about Charlie Parker and tricksters in Jazz music provides a new way of seeing both Jazz and the trickster archetype in American culture. I am honored to have been asked to write this foreword, given his prolific research history on this musical genre. The Trickster is a fascinating topic and character transcending Jazz and American culture. It does have notable variations, but something common across societies and cultures persists. When asking what the nature of this archetype is, my first thoughts are whether the trickster is a socially interactional creation implicitly suggesting a potential for being a trickster in many of us. Although interactions are pivotal to its social recognition by others, the trickster has to reach beyond loosely connected situations.

Do certain circumstances therefore correspond with the displayed and patterned "doings" (West and Zimmerman 1987) associated with the trickster character or archetype? What are the potential processes of becoming a trickster? Is there a definable set of characteristics of being a trickster within jazz that differs from other contexts, scenes, or subcultures? These are difficult questions warranting more research and indicative of the depth of this engaging topic; however, good and sound research understands its limitations of scope and purpose. This book provides a very thoughtful, rich, and empirical engagement of Charlie Parker, tricksters and how they pertain not only to jazz, but also to American culture and its historical inequalities and divisions related to African Americans.

I will not pretend to know jazz like Frank Salamone. I know Charlie Parker as a distanced fan of his amazing musical talent, importance to the inception of bebop, and having the posthumous ability to scare a young high school musician with his practice scales for bass clef instruments. That tuba player was me. On reflection, the experience was a possible introduction to a "symbolic boundary" (Lamont and Fournier 1992), distinguishing a different and much higher musical aptitude, education and subculture. As Salamone thoroughly discusses, the creation and construction of boundaries are an almost essential prerequisite to this contentious character. It is the trickster's *raison d'être* to violate, challenge, and usurp not only symbolic, but also social boundaries. Potentially, little is sacrosanct, and a "biting humor" with a notable reflexivity is almost a requirement for jazz musicians and tricksters.

For the sake of theoretical comparisons we may consider a few other relevant "character types" or social roles within the scope of unequal social class and racial relations. David Riesman spoke of an "autonomous person" in his renowned, yet somewhat forgotten book *The Lonely Crowd*, first published in 1950. The autonomous type questions and does not adjust to the predominant mode of conformity and authority of their respective time period. The autonomous type resists, including to the preferences of their "peer group", due at least partially to their heightened "self-consciousness" (Riesman 2001:255-259). From Salamone's description, the jazz trickster is also similar to an "organic intellectual". Antonio Gramsci describes this role within the ongoing class conflict and bourgeois domination in capitalism. These grassroots intellectuals are organically born from the classes and groups marginalized, alienated and oppressed. These agents help mobilize "counter-hegemonic" forces and collective actions to uproot and destabilize the control and oppressive forms of authority. Much like these tricksters, they can use their charisma, musical talent, and deep understanding of the social circumstances to solidify their impact (Storey 2009:88-91).

Frank Salamone's tour of the jazz trickster makes many fascinating stops. Charlie Parker is ostensibly at the root of this book, but many of the famous and prolific jazz masters that "Bird" was connected to formed a dream-like social network. Louis Armstrong, Dizzy Gillespie and Charles Mingus are a few of the major figures Salamone discusses in terms of having influenced or played with Charlie Parker during his shortened, but potent, life. These musicians in addition to others, like Miles Davis, also challenged the *status quo* of the dominant white class and culture. He retells a few stories where Dizzy Gillespie injects subversive humor to both recognize racial inequalities and the civil rights issues of the time and places. The jazz trickster acts with greater autonomy recklessly transgressing and reconstructing through deconstruction. This also unavoidably teaches observers by raising awareness and social consciousness.

As for the role of a teacher, there are many possible lessons from the jazz tricksters. The trickster challenges the accepted definition of the situation or "frame" (Goffman 1986:10) with the help of humor. The arbitrariness of traditionally accepted boundaries is illuminated. Much like the cultural jamming of today, the trickster, teaches through challenging political power structures. Ironically, the jazz "jam session" (Cameron 1954) was an important sessional technique and format within the jazz subculture where imagination and musical improvisation is paramount. Salamone recognizes the importance of the imagination for the trickster and his agency. Imaginative improvisation, as noted by Salamone, teaches through representation how jazz musicians responded to the racial oppression of the Jim Crow south.

In his book *Stigma*, Erving Goffman slyly and eloquently demonstrates how many people are seemingly normal, but secretly deviant, using the term "normal deviants" to define this "feature of society" (Goffman 1963:130). The jazz trickster embodies and uncovers these social and cultural contradictions that comprise many of us. We are potentially "hip" and "squares" (Becker 1963:90), but some cultures and subcultures have a long history of producing these cultural characters as responses to bigger societal injustices. By showing this arbitrariness, the jazz tricksters taught their greatest lessons about societal inequalities and social and symbolic boundaries and structures, *vis-à-vis* transgression. Salamone brings to life the relationships and influences between Charlie Parker, other famous jazzmen and the larger cultural characteristics symbolized in the black and African American experiences. This is a very worthwhile and enjoyable addition to the study of tricksters and Jazz music and subculture.

Marcus Aldredge
Assistant Professor of Sociology
Iona College
New Rochelle, NY

Works Cited

Becker, Howard S. 1963. *Outsiders: Studies in the Sociology of Deviance.* New York: Free Press.
Cameron, William Bruce. 1954. "Sociological Notes on the Jam Session." *Social Forces*, 33(2):177-82.
Gofffman, Erving. 1963. *Stigma: Notes on the Management of Spoiled Identity.* New York: Simon &Schuster.
Goffman, Erving. [1974] 1986. *Frame Analysis: An Essay on the Organization of Experience.* Boston: Northeastern University Press.

Lamont, Michele and Marcel Fournier, eds. 1992. *Cultivating Differences: Symbolic Boundaries and the making of Inequality.* Chicago, IL: University of Chicago Press.
Riesman, David, Nathan Glazer and Reuel Denney. [1950] 2001. *The Lonely Crowd.* New Haven, CT Yale University Press.
Storey, John. 2009. "Rockin' Hegemony: West Coast Rock and Amerika's War in Vietnam." Pp. 88-97 in *Cultural Theory and Popular Culture*, edited by John Storey. Harlow, UK: Pearson Education Ltd.
West, Candace and Don H. Zimmerman. 1987. *Gender & Society*, 1(2):125-151.

Acknowledgements

I wish to thank all those musicians who taught me about jazz through taking the time to talk to me, including Hugh Lawson, Matty Ross, Dizzy Gillespie, Jimmy Heath, Larry Luger, Frank Foster, Kaef Ruzaden, Fela, Richard Schulman, Benny Powell, Ali Ryerson, Peter King, Danny Mixon, and so many more. These discussions took place in the United States, Nigeria, and the United Kingdom. Most thanks go to my wife who has patiently accompanied me on many occasions and listened to my overheated rants on jazz, and how people do not properly understand or appreciate it, and the nuances in the art of different musicians. She encouraged me to listen to how much wisdom and intelligence went into their comments and views on life. Thanks, Virginia for being my muse.

INTRODUCTION

I have been a jazz fan for over 60 years. My Uncle Jake took me to pick up some relatives of his at a club in Rochester called the Golden Grill near Lake Ontario one Sunday. I waited in the outer lobby while he went in. The moment he opened the door I was in heaven. I remember asking him what that music was called. He laughed in the usual way and said, "That's jazz." I was hooked. Oh sure, I had heard jazz since I was born in 1939. It was on the radio daily. It was in the movies frequently. Juke boxes were filled with it. I had, however, never heard "live jazz". When that door opened letting my uncle into the club, I felt as if the gates of heaven had opened and Gabriel was playing the horn. Surely, that music must be the soundtrack of paradise. It was a moment that changed my life.

Later I realized that what I had heard was called Dixieland jazz or New Orleans jazz, maybe even Chicago jazz, trad jazz, moldy fig or even classic jazz, depending on the time, place, or person doing the classifying. As I grew older, I knew that all kinds of jazz were simply jazz, and came from Louis Armstrong, no matter what they were called. Louis never tried to avoid the term, as some jazz greats did. Ellington, for example, who was a bit older than Louis, stated that there was simply good music and the rest. The very good was beyond category. I know what the Duke of Ellington was saying, and I can dig it. However, he knew what he played was jazz whatever else he or someone else called it.

I knew that I wanted to play that music. I never really could. Oh, there were two or three times I actually did. As jazz musicians say, something played my instrument through me on those occasions. One was an impromptu school dance in junior high. The other was at a club as an adult when I started taking lessons again. That was really it. But it was enough to help give me a glimpse of what the transcendent realm of the spiritual is like, to be in the eternal now, and to be totally lost. Two or three brief moments in a long life may not seem like much, but they are enough.

Indeed the high E-flat on my alto sax that brought a crowd to its feet and turned the heads of professional musicians and the eighth and ninth grade kids dancing and roaring their approval in the early 1950s while I played music was something I could never again duplicate. Nevertheless, they were enough for me to understand why Charlie Parker, Dizzy Gillespie, Fela, Bill Evans, Duke Ellington and many other jazz-based musicians stated that jazz is spiritual. Parker went farther than anyone else, and declared that jazz was his religion. Indeed, Coltrane also used jazz to get in touch with his own spirituality.

I had to distill my own spirituality from listening to jazz. Not all jazz brought me to the absolute heights. Truly, some jazz was bad. Most was mediocre, like most of life itself. But even the mediocre had its surprises. The level of music of the greats is indeed high. It goes beyond technical competence to a realm that is indeed far, far away. Even when Bird Parker was not at his best, it was better than all but a few. In his declining years Satchmo Armstrong could bring a chill before the night was past. Coltrane, the great Trane, would thrill you even when playing his squeaks and squawks in the mid to late 1960s. Dizzy, suffering from cancer of the jaw, would prove now and then that he was among the giants. Monk with his angular and strange music fought off his inner demons to provide magical moments. And on it went.

I found that most musicians—indeed, all but one—would talk freely about their mystical experience. The Yoruba Trickster himself, Fela Anakulapi Kuti, the man who carried death in his pocket, spoke freely to me in Lagos at his club, The Shrine, about the spirituality of Black Music. As he puffed on his marijuana joint, he waxed eloquent about the spirituality of his music. It was his sacred calling, his destiny. I could multiply the examples but the point is clear, that the music is sacred and spiritual.

It also, like Fela, speaks truth to power, to the squares that control the world and pile up their unfair share of its goods. Louis Armstrong put his career on the line to oppose segregation and call out the President of the United States on his failure to enforce the law equally. He called on Dwight D. (Ike) Eisenhower to go with him to Selma, Alabama, and take the first little black child he saw by the hand and walk into the school house. Dizzy sang about segregation and fought it with humor. He sang, "I'll never go back to Georgia. No, I'll never go back to Georgia", putting that line in the middle of "Swing Low, Sweet Cadillac", itself a parody of "Swing Low, Sweet Chariot". That song was based on a Yoruba song. And so it goes.

The music is one that refers to anything and everything in one's life. Nothing human is foreign to it. The juxtaposition of the incongruous, the sign of the trickster, is the meat of jazz, especially among those who are more than the merely great, as Jeff Goldblum's character in the movie "Lush Life", noted. Biting humor is an earmark of jazz. Musicians make themselves the butt of jokes. It gets them past their pain, through their long nights before uncomprehending and rude fans. It gets them past their bitterness at seeing lesser musicians making more money playing square and simple tunes. They will tell you the joke about the fool who played jazz for the money.

For every Miles Davis or Dave Brubeck, there are many outstanding jazz musicians who barely make their car payments. There are too many who die in poverty. I hung around for many years with great musicians. I have kept in touch with a few. Jimmy Heath still greets me, as does Gary Smulyan. Others nod to me. A number want me to be their agent. Indeed, I did so with one musician, Larry Luger, a fine guitarist. He said I was the only one who kept my promises. I got him gigs and wrote articles about him, as promised. I stopped working for him when I went to Nigeria on a Fulbright.

Almost nothing else in life, except my parents, my wife, my kids and grandkids, and great-grandson, has given me so much joy and pleasure. Every time I play Sonny Rollins, Bud Powell, and, of course, Bird, Satchmo and Diz, I am no longer in this world. I see things more clearly, with greater perspective. Only Mozart gives me as much pure joy and pleasure among composers. I wish there had been some means of recording his improvisations. I think if he were alive, he would be going to a gig tonight, bitching about the crappy out of tune piano he would have to play tonight, but he would do so with a smile and impish gleam in his eye.

Chapter One

Charlie Parker— Bird Lives!

"Music is your own experience, your own thoughts, your wisdom. If you don't live it, it won't come out of your horn. They teach you there's a boundary line to music. But, man, there's no boundary line to art."
—As quoted in *Bird: The Legend of Charlie Parker* (1977), by Robert George Reisner, p.27

"Louis Armstrong, Charlie Parker."
—Miles Davis summarizing the history of jazz

Introduction

Charles Mingus, the legendary and troubled genius of the bass and composition, issued an album in 1957 entitled "The Clown". Jean Shepherd did the narration for the title song. In it, Mingus's meaning is clarified. The clown of the title is none other than the jazz performer himself. Certainly, Mingus had himself in mind but he also meant to apply it to others, and certainly to Charlie Parker whom Mingus idolized, writing "Reincarnation of a Lovebird" for this album. Shepherd's narration includes a section indicating that only when the clown accidentally falls and injures himself does he achieve great popularity. He cashes in on that popularity, inserting his message behind the tricks, an apt metaphor for the tricksters in jazz. Indeed, it is no accident that the two major tricksters in jazz, Louis Armstrong and Charlie Parker, were trickster, and both not so incidentally were influences on Mingus.

Trickster

In mythology and religion, the trickster deity breaks the rules of the gods or nature, sometimes maliciously but usually, albeit unintentionally, with ultimately positive effects. Often, the bending/breaking of rules takes the form of tricks or thievery. Tricksters can be cunning or foolish or both; they are often funny even when considered sacred or performing important cultural tasks.[1]

Although Trickster is found in many different cultures, the first full anthropological description of a trickster figure was found in Paul Radin's study of Native Americans, *The Trickster: A Study in American Indian Mythology* (1987, originally 1955). Subsequently, many other studies of Trickster followed. Lewis Hyde's tour de force, *Trickster Makes the World*, comes closest to what I am trying to convey here. The *Kirkus Review* notes that Hyde "delineates some of their common themes: voracious appetite, ingenious theft, deceit, opportunism, and shamelessness. Through such themes trickster tales dramatize a mythic consciousness of accident and contingency (supplementing fate), moral ambiguity, foolishness, and transgression—in other words, the world as it is, rather than the way it may originally have been intended by the more senior gods". Trickster in art is a mighty force for creativity through change of the status quo.

---

[1] TV Tropes: http://tvtropes.org/pmwiki/pmwiki.php/Main/TheTrickster?from=Main.Trickstes.

Additionally, note the common themes of Trickster. Trickster has an incredible appetite, whether it is food, sex, or mind-altering substances. He is a shameless thief, crafty in his deceit but albeit loveable and creative. He is noted for mocking these gods, jumping on accident and opportunity to come up with something new, maybe better than what came before, and maybe not. In sum, Trickster is a boundary crosser. He apparently is unable to resist finding out what is on the other side. Trickster seemingly must subvert boundaries and present the moral ambiguity present in the world. The *Kirkus Review* article of Hyde's work uses Stephen Douglass as a model. Douglass certainly is an apt model for African American tricksters like Parker, who defied many seemingly rigid ethnic, artistic, marital, conventional moral and segregationist boundaries, dying in the New York apartment of the Jazz Baroness, Kathleen Annie Pannonica Rothschild de Koenigswarter (known as "Nica").

Bird

When Charlie Parker died the phrase "Bird Lives!" was found scrawled on walls all over New York City. March 12, 1955 was a sad day for those who loved bebop, modern jazz, or just plain great art. The phrase captured both the sadness and the realization that in some way Charlie Parker, known as Bird, would live on. While there may have been those who refused to believe the fact of his physical death, there were many more who knew his music would continue into the future, breaking boundaries along the way. It is, after all, the obligation of tricksters to shatter boundaries and bring about change, to be beyond category, and to live their own idiosyncratic lives.

African American culture is marked by tricksterism, and black music has had no lack of tricksters. Arguably, Parker and Louis Armstrong have been the greatest of them all. Parker paid his tribute to Armstrong in memorizing many of his solos note for note and then performing them within his own improvisations, although usually at greater speeds. Both, however, shared a knack for transforming other music into new music with a personal stamp on it.

In his article, "The Years with Yard", Dizzy Gillespie (2009:82-84) notes both his trickster-like quality and his ability to transform music into something beyond the ordinary while revealing its essence. He notes that Parker had the ability to play rapidly but also melodiously, because his deep knowledge of harmony allowed him always to find the melody in the harmony. He says that in his opinion Parker may not have been aware of twenty-five per cent of what he played; it just came out of his being and fell under his fingers. That view may have come from Parker's own saying, "Don't play the saxophone. Let it play you." Parker had also stated that the secret of playing was to learn all you could about your instrument and then forgot all that and just play.

There is something almost mystical and certainly nearly Zen-like in these statements. Parker often took both sides of various issues, sometimes in the same interview, often in different interviews.[2]

Did he have influences from earlier jazz musicians? Is be-bop part of jazz? Did he know that what he was playing was something new? It all depends on which interview you read or listen to. In all his interviews, he was deferential to a fault. It is not hard to know that he was puttin' on old Massa. Now and then he would address something head on, but by then there was so much smoke it was hard to tell. To be sure, one has to go to Dizzy Gillespie's writings and interviews (for example, Gillespie 2009a and b, among others). There, Dizzy lays out the connections of be-bop to earlier jazz and the influences of various players on Bird. In his Blindfold Test with Leonard Feather, Bird reveals his vast knowledge of earlier styles as well as his love for them (Leonard Feather: A Bird's-ear View of Music. Nobody gets the bird from Bird as broadminded Parker takes the blindfold test, in Metronome, 64/8 (Aug.1948), p.14, 21-22).

There is no doubt that Bird inhaled the work of Louis Armstrong. Kevin Young has much to say about both men and their relationship to each other in terms of being tricksters. He says this about Armstrong: "... for innovators like Louis Armstrong, who also saw themselves as showmen, entertainer is no less a mask than cool is for those who came later" (2012:198).

In a broader context, Armstrong's trickster role can be tied to the jazz musical genre that he so transformed. Both were subject to—and responded to—unavoidable social realities, expressing pain and anger in reaction to a debilitating racism. Both also employed secret musical codes, employing protective masks that gave space to individual freedom and collective empowerment. Furthermore, both recognized humor as the license that permitted their liberationist expressions of thinly veiled social commentary. Jazz, like Armstrong, offered a language, the subtleties of which spoke *to* the in-crowd (the "hip") and *about* the outsiders (the "squares"). Invariably, it would privately mock either or both. Iain Ellis (October 2005) refers to one of my writings to summarize this point:

---

[2] See Michael Levin and John S. Wilson 2009: 32-36; Leonard Feather http://www.melmartin.com/html_pages/interviews.html.
Paul Desmond 1954: http://www.melmartin.com/html_pages/interviews.html.

Critic Frank A. Salamone adeptly analyzed the trickster humor at work in Armstrong's popular song, "Laughin' Louie". Firstly, the "squares" are outed in the title itself, which parodies the common misinterpretation of his name in mainstream culture and mocks the one-dimensional stereotype with which he was regarded (and sometimes dismissed). From Armstrong's point-of-view, the title's humor might also allude to his habitual pot-smoking habits, this further underscored by the name of his accompanying band, the Vipers, a slang term for marijuana. The song's music fluctuates throughout, between the "hot" sound "hip" critics encouraged from Armstrong, and the "sweet" sounds he always had such affection for, but for which he was criticized as compromising to mainstream tastes. Here, the trickster celebrates his own creative choices (laughing for himself), and satirically dismisses the imposing judgment of his critics (laughing at them). This is achieved through the humorous method of incongruity, the shock of the juxtaposed styles surprising listeners into recognition and appreciation.

We can safely say that both Armstrong and Parker are exemplars of the trickster in jazz, even if they are so in different ways. However, we need to delve more deeply into what we mean by Trickster and what role he plays in African American culture, particularly jazz.

His (Hyde's) choice of the fiery nineteenth century African American orator Frederick Douglass may at first seem puzzling in this regard. But in light of the real-life gravity of the "boundaries Douglass crossed, and the ingenuity with which he did so", Hyde's example makes sense. Indeed, with his clever interpretive skills and his eye for the meaning-rich detail, Hyde brightly illuminates the ways in which his examples struggled to subvert such seemingly intractable elements as the definition of art or slavery and segregation (*Kirkus Reviews*. LXV, November 1, 1997, p. 1623).

Trickster, then, is a boundary-crosser, subverting conventional boundaries. Trickster's very subversion of conventional boundaries opens up new vistas, new ways of seeing and thinking. Once thought and shown, these new ways seem "right", almost obvious, and equivalent to Kuhn's concept of paradigm shift (Thomas S. Kuhn, *The Structure of Scientific Revolutions* 1996).

In an interview with Paul Desmond and John McLellan, Parker was asked about his revolutionary change in music. After responding that he did not know that he was doing anything that much different from others, he elaborated on what he fundamentally was doing:

But I mean, ever since I've ever heard music I've thought it should be very clean, very precise—as clean as possible anyway, you know. And more or less to the people, you know something they could understand. Something that was beautiful, you know. There's definitely stories and stories and stories that can be told in the musical idiom, you know. You wouldn't say idiom but it's so hard to describe music other than the basic way to describe it—music is basically melody, harmony, and rhythm. But, I mean people can do much more with music than that. It can be very descriptive in all kinds of ways, you know, all walks of life (Paul Desmond interviews Charlie Parker 1954).

Parker clearly sees his music as crossing boundaries and having clear implications for "all walks of life". He has stories to tell. The technical trappings of music are there to help one tell stories, to comment on life, and to break through restrictions.

Gerry Mulligan notes how he, and by extension his generation of players experienced Bird's music:

> ... when Bird played it was like a new country had been heard from. It just was an altogether different atmosphere and it was really striking because he played with such clarity ...[3]

For some people that was not a good thing. Many older jazz musicians termed the music "Chinese", by which slur they meant that it was dissonant in sound and that there was no clarity of cohesion in it. While that may have been true of some of the bop musicians, it was not true of Parker. His music was always tonal, logical, steeped in the blues and clear. It was simply telling a different story than most other musicians, even than that of his close collaborators, like Dizzy Gillespie.

The strong negative reaction to his music by many older people and others who preferred more pop oriented music is not surprising. That in no way lessened his impact. His influence was felt even in Dixieland bands, or more accurately in New Orleans and Swing music. Jon Hendricks, the poet laureate of jazz, poked fun at the moldy figs. He wrote in his lyrics to *Everybody's Boppin'*:

> Bop ain't dead, that's a line o' jive,
> Dixieland bands done kept it alive.
> Tell that square to take a dive,
> 'Cause everybody's boppin'. (Columbia: 1989, reissue)

---

[3] Autobiography:
http://lcweb4.loc.gov/natlib/ihas/service/mulligan/100010952/0001.pdf.

There is a close relationship between the deep structure of both musics. It took the genius of a Charlie Parker to bring it out in the open and show it in a new light. Perhaps that only added to the strong negative reaction Bird faced among many established older musicians. I mean his ability to transform even the great solos of Louis Armstrong into something rediscovered. Armstrong, usually generous toward other musicians, took some time warming up to Dizzy Gillespie, who became a close friend and frequent visitor at Louis's home. Interestingly, Armstrong never did say anything good about Bird that I have found. Rather, he delighted in telling a story about how Charlie Parker had to be dragged on the stage at a festival in France after Sidney Bechet had finished playing. It sounds very close to the story told of how Lester Young had to be pushed onstage after Bird's solo at a *Jazz at the Philharmonic* concert. I do not believe either story.

Thus, like most tricksters, Parker rearranged the world while challenging people's understanding of what they had taken for granted. He recombined material from the past, made it new, and saw others rework his material. He could play with older and younger musicians with ease. He was never easy to pin down, as interviews with him demonstrate very clearly. His personal life was rarely as orderly as his art. Chaotic is the best word to describe it. It was filled with unresolved contradictions. Bird was a man of great appetites, which finally led to his demise. And yet, as the graffiti on the walls of New York buildings proclaimed, Bird Lives.

Conclusion

Everywhere one looks among premodern peoples, there are tricky mythical beings alike enough to entice any human mind to create a category for them once it had met two or three. They are beings of the beginning, working in some complex relationship with the High God; transformers, helping to bring the present human world into being; performers of heroic acts on behalf of men, yet in their original form. Or, in some later form, foolish, obscene, laughable, yet indomitable (Robert D. Pelton, *The Trickster in West Africa*, 15).

Do the times make the man, or does the man make the times? Bird came along at a time jazz was sounding tired. The World War helped bring black protest into the open again, after it had died away during the Depression and general hard times, or at least went underground, and a new generation of African Americans began to express themselves, exploiting the contradictions in American life revealed by the war. These two forces came together and provided the soil from which bebop sprang. Charlie Parker grew up in the twin Kansas Cities. That the Twin Cities' music was steeped in blues provided a link between swing and bop and fostered many types of fusion in jazz.

Bird himself was a charismatic person, filled with contradictions. He was erudite, but could act in childish ways. He longed for recognition from "serious" musicians, playing with a string section on recordings and at clubs, most notably Birdland, a club named after him but from which he was ultimately barred. He was innocently surprised when someone asked him if he was paid for the use of his name. Like Trickster, Bird was filled with contradictions. This description of Trickster could be a description of Charlie Parker.

Trickster is the mythic embodiment of ambiguity and ambivalence, doubleness and duplicity, contradiction and paradox (7), and can thus be seen as the archetypal boundary-crosser, although here Hyde notes that "there are also cases in which trickster creates a boundary, or brings to the surface a distinction previously hidden from sight" (7).

Bird indeed crossed numerous boundaries. Bebop may at first sound dissonant, but it really is not when one analyses the chords, especially their higher intervals. It is a new way of looking at music. It is deeply rooted in jazz in spite of early criticism, and even goes back to early New Orleans jazz in ways swing usually did not. It provided a bridge to later forms of jazz, which in my view do not have its verve or depth. Wynton Marsalis has said many times that it is the hardest type of jazz to play. Bird stated many times that he wanted to study with Hindemith, and that Hindemith had agreed to take him on as a student. While many of his followers derided Louis Armstrong and classical music, not the better of them to be sure, Bird slipped in solos based on *The Firebird* and improvisation on Satchmo's *West End Blues*. According to Dizzy Gillespie (Salamone 1990a) Bird was at home with African music whose rhythms suited his tastes.

Not only was he an embodiment of Trickster in his professional and personal life, he was the personification of Walt Whitman's American (Whitman's *Song of Myself*). He did indeed contradict himself, and did contain multitudes. The times could not and did not tolerate him. The harassment of New York's finest and their drug busts targeting bop musicians, the virulent racism of the times, the slurs of many, not all, established musicians, the copy-cats singled out in Charlie Mingus's musical tributes to Bird, all helped lead to his death. They also served to make him a martyr and to help perpetuate his music. Charlie Parker, the Trickster, did indeed cross many boundaries, and people are still working out his changes.

Coda

I saw Charlie Parker once. It was at a Jazz at the Philharmonic concert in Rochester, NY, in 1954 or 1955. I was a young teen, in love with jazz and awed by the stories I had read of Bird. I had heard some of his music, but not a lot. Still, it was enough to whet my appetite. I was surprised when Bird came on stage. He did not have his own group but was backed, so my memory tells me, by the Oscar Peterson Trio. Despite its name, there was also a drummer with the trio: with Bird, that made it a quintet.

That was not the main surprise. Bird was disheveled and seemed disoriented. He had a baggy suit on, was overweight, and his horn looked shopworn. However, when he put the horn to his lips, closed his eyes and blew, the surprise was that a "gentleman bum", in George Shearing's words, could make such music (Salamone 1990b). I had taken sax and clarinet lessons, but knew very little music theory at that time. I only knew that I was witnessing a force of nature. Music that down-to-earth but also ethereal could only come from a complicated individual.

Shearing had told me that Bird, looking like a "gentleman bum", was the only musician who approached him in Birdland, asking if Shearing wanted to go outside for a walk. He helped George on with his coat and unobtrusively guided him out the door. Shearing said that Bird frequently made little gestures like that, which contradicted the stories that made him out to be unaware of others and totally self-absorbed (cf, for example,

Miles Davis, 1990). There are, of course, other stories of Bird's kindness, such as his giving Davis a free place to stay, and sponsoring his career when many other musicians wondered why he bothered with the rich kid from East St. Louis.

When all these stories are put together, the contradictions, the wit, charm, intelligence, excesses and appetite with a skill that seems to have come from nowhere and influenced the future of the music as only Louis Armstrong had done, we have a portrait of a consummate trickster. His untimely death adds to the legend, as do stories of bird feathers floating from the heavens on the day he died. I have spoken with some of his very close friends about him—Dizzy Gillespie, who said Bird was the other beat of his heart, and Bob Redcross, for whom Bird wrote a song of the same name and who was a general factotum and who swore that Bird could pick up any wind instrument and play it perfectly the first time. They all note his contradictory nature and his charm. He was indeed the personification of Trickster, and, like Trickster, he self-destructed.

References

Charlie Parker – Koko
http://www.youtube.com/watch?v=okrNwE6GI70&feature=related

Davis, Miles. Miles: The Autobiography. Simon & Schuster; 1rst Preston Edition. 1990

Desmond, Paul Paul Desmond Interviews Charlie Parker. This is a radio broadcast from early 1954 (probably March) in Boston, Mass. with announcer John McLellan.

Ellis, Iain. Laughin' Louie. http://www.popmatters.com/pm/column/ellis051013/ Accessed May 3, 2012

Feather, Leonard: A Bird's-ear View of Music. Nobody gets the bird from bird as broadminded parker takes the blindfold test, in: Metronome, 64/8 (Aug.1948), p. 14, 21-22

Harrison, Paul Carter, Victor Leo Walker II, Gus Edward Black Theater: Ritual Performance in the African Diaspora. Philadelphia: Temple University Press, 2002

Hyde, Lewis. Trickster Makes This World: Mischief, Myth, and Art. Berkeley: North Point Press, 1997.

Kirkus Reviews. LXV, November 1, 1997, p. 1623.

Kuhn, Thomas S. *The Structure of Scientific Revolutions.* Chicago and London: University of Chicago Press, 1996 (3rd Ed.)

Mulligan, Gerry. Autobiography. http://lcweb4.loc.gov/natlib/ihas/service/mulligan/100010952/0001.pdf 1995.

Radin, Paul. The Trickster: A Study in American Indian Mythology. New York: Schocken. 1985, original 1955.

Pelton, Robert D. The Trickster in West Africa. Berkeley: University of California Press, 1989.

Salamone, Frank A. "The Force Primeval: An Image of Jazz in American Literature." Play & Culture. 3(3):256-266, 1990a

—. "George Shearing: Interview." Cadence. 16(4):5-8, 24, 1990b

—. "Laughin' Louie: An Analysis of Louis Armstrong's Record and its Relationship to African-American Musical Humor." Humor: International Journal of Humor Research 15.1 (2002):47-64.

TV Tropes http://tvtropes.org/pmwiki/pmwiki.php/Main/TheTrickster?from=Main.Tricksters first Accessed May 5, 2012

Whitman, Walt. Whitman's *Song of Myself.* http://www.english.illinois.edu/maps/poets/s_z/whitman/song.htm first Accessed October 25, 2012

CHAPTER TWO

THE TRANSFORMATIVE POWER OF JAZZ: TRICKSTER AND HIS ROLE IN JAZZ

"I think his sense of humor lets him get away with things the rest of us wouldn't have the nerve to try".
—Attributed to Phil Woods and Gene Lees.

"I am too famous to die."
—Dizzy Gillespie on his deathbed.

[The trickster] is a forerunner of the saviour... He is both subhuman and superhuman, a bestial and divine being, whose chief and most alarming characteristic is his unconsciousness.
"On the Psychology of the Trickster-Figure," Carl Jung CW 9i, par. 472.

The role of the trickster in African culture is well-known (Frederick-Malanson 2012; Badejo 1988; Ugorji 1991; Gates 1988; Hyde 1998; Jung; Davis 1991). He is a dangerous character, one who changes and transforms reality. Seemingly off-handedly he creates and recreates the world. If he were not filled with humor, it is debatable whether anyone would ever approach him. Certainly, there have been figures in African, and west African, culture that fulfill the role of Trickster. Musicians come quite easily to mind. I will name two, one African and one African American, namely, Fela, the Nigerian rebel musician, and Dizzy Gillespie, one of the creators of be-bop who also used humor to makes dangerous points, points that upset the status quo.

However, the proper place for trickster figures is religion. Indeed, both Fela and Gillespie saw their music as spiritual, as each man told me (Salamone 2008). Shamans and priests in west Africa often partake of trickster characteristics. In mythology and religion, the trickster deity breaks the rules of the gods or nature, sometimes maliciously but usually, albeit unintentionally, with ultimately positive effects. Often, the bending/breaking of rules takes the form of tricks or thievery. Tricksters can be cunning or foolish or both; they are often funny even when considered sacred or performing important cultural tasks.

Charles Mingus, the legendary and troubled genius of the bass and composition, issued an album in 1957 entitled "The Clown". Jean Shepherd did the narration for the title song. In it, Mingus's meaning is clarified. The title clown is none other than the jazz performer himself. Certainly, Mingus had himself in mind but he also meant to apply it to others, and certainly to Charlie Parker, whom Mingus idolized, writing "Reincarnation of a Lovebird" for this album. Shepherd's narration includes a section indicating that only when the clown accidentally falls and injures himself does he achieve great popularity. He cashes in on that popularity, inserting his message behind the tricks, an apt metaphor for the tricksters in jazz. Indeed, it is no accident that the two major tricksters in jazz, Louis Armstrong and Charlie Parker, were trickster, and both not-so-incidentally were influences on Mingus.

In mythology and religion, the trickster deity breaks the rules of the gods or nature, sometimes maliciously but usually, albeit unintentionally, with ultimately positive effects. Often, the bending/breaking of rules takes the form of tricks or thievery. Tricksters can be cunning or foolish or both; they are often funny even when considered sacred or performing important cultural tasks.[4]

African American culture is marked by tricksterism, and black music has had no lack of tricksters. Arguably, Parker and Louis Armstrong have been the greatest of them all. Parker paid his tribute to Armstrong in memorizing many of his solos note for note and then performing them within his own improvisations, although usually at greater speeds. Both, however, shared a knack for transforming other music into new music with a personal stamp on it.

The Diz and Tricksters

Trickster myth is found in clearly recognizable form among both aboriginal tribes and modern societies. We encounter it among the ancient Greeks, Chinese, and the Japanese and in the Semitic world as well. Many of the trickster's traits were perpetuated in the figure of the mediæval jester, and survived right up to the present day in the Punch and Judy plays and in the clown. Although repeatedly combined with other myths and frequently drastically reorganized and reinterpreted, its basic plot seems

---

[4] TV Tropes: http://tvtropes.org/pmwiki/pmwiki.php/Main/TheTrickster?from=Main.Tricksters.

always to have succeeded in reasserting itself (Radin 1955:ix).

We have a fundamental figure here, which is both general and specific. There appears a general need for the trickster, but a need clothed in specific features of a culture. The trickster can be creator and destroyer, one who gives and one who takes, one who tricks and is tricked. The trickster inspires awe and affection at the same time. Seemingly, the trickster is one who gives into primal impulses without thinking; but I would argue that he is sly as a fox, who does, at least at times, clearly see the results of his behavior, but who can get away with much because of his humor.

I have argued that powerful, sacred African figures require humor so that the audience can approach them (Salamone 1995:3-7; Salamone 1976: 08-210). The informality prevalent in most American jazz allows the royalty to temper the awe inherent in their status in order to permit youngsters to approach them. I suggest that much the same practice can be found in Nigeria. For example, I worked with a traditional priest who was one of the more powerful "doctors" in Nigeria. However, in order to encourage clients he appeared in a somewhat worn robe and acted the clown. When I asked him about the meaning of jazz, he replied with his usual arch wit that it was spiritual because it makes the other fellow sound *good*. Additionally, there is an African tradition which holds that the musician has a sacred duty to stand up to oppression and speak the truth to power. In that task, Gillespie followed a long tradition of African musicians. It is no accident, I think, that the Yoruba musician Fela Anakulapi-Kuti studied and worked with Gillespie early in his career. Even Fela's claim to be the Black President has traces of Gillespie's half-humorous presidential candidacy. Fela combined various aspects of African-based music into his style. Interestingly, its foundation was the jazz of Gillespie and Charlie Parker, which he heard as a young man and which he used to create something different for Nigerian music, something he deemed would be revolutionary. He put on a mask of the trickster to perform, mocking those whom he deemed had betrayed Africa, the colonialists and their African collaborators.

The Humor of Subversion

Dizzy would often open his performances by saying he would like to introduce the band. Band members would then turn to one another and shake hands, giving their names to each other while smiling and nodding. The routine, which I saw repeated many times, never got stale. Diz would sometimes stand aside and raise his eyebrows bemusedly at the audience.

Eventually, he would get to introduce the musicians in the band, for Diz was a fair man who gave each person his due.

I remember one night in 1957-58 when he arrived in the middle of a blizzard to perform in Rochester, NY. He was late, something unusual for him. The audience, however, waited for him, knowing that somehow he'd make it through the storm. In those days, Diz traveled by car around the Birdland Circuit, and he was coming in from Detroit. As the band scrambled to take off their heavy, snow-laden coats and assemble their instruments, Diz began to play solo trumpet.

The audience laughed as they recognized a current hit, "Tequila", by the Champs. They stopped laughing when they realized Diz had bested them again because he was playing it straight. He took the novelty tune and reimagined it as a lovely, then torrid, Latin tune. One by one the band members joined in as they assembled their instruments.

After ten minutes or so, Diz then began his spiel. He apologized for being late: "I was playing a benefit for the Ku Klux Klan at the White Citizens' Hall in Montgomery Alabama." As the crowd broke up with laughter, he launched into "Manteca" (Grease) with his new opening chant, "I'll never go back to Georgia. No, I'll never go back to Georgia". Again, as the crowd—and it was a crowd, despite the snow—roared with laughter, he launched into a brilliant high-note solo, complete with all the pyrotechnics of which he was capable in his prime.

I reminded Diz of this performance thirty years later when he was performing at Elizabeth Seton College. He remembered it with a smile and vocally repeated the opening of his solo for me. It was then that he talked about humor and the spirituality of music, among many other topics. Diz took his role as a teacher/musician seriously, reminding me of Chaucer's scholar: "Gladly would he learn and gladly teach".

There was another routine he had when doing "Swing Low, Sweet Cadillac", his version of "Swing Low, Sweet Chariot". The song is not just an American spiritual, but comes from an African religious song. Diz began his version with a Yoruba chant from Chano Pozo, a Cuban Santeria (a member of an Afro-Cuban religious group based on Yoruba religious principles). The chant often drew befuddled laughs from the audience, and Diz played it up big. For him, humor and spirituality were not polar opposites but complementary principles. Humor was a means of leading people to the spiritual.

As he told me, "When Chano Pozo came, the music all came together." Again, once Diz finished his chanting, also setting the cross-rhythms of his tempo, he started the song, in the midst of which he took a brilliant solo. When the tenor sax player James Moody was present, there would be two brilliant solos. Then the piece would end with Dizzy's tag line, "Old Cadillacs never die. The finance company just tows them away!"

The examples could continue. Just what was this once wild bad boy of jazz getting at? What did his great dancing in front of his band mean? His mugging with his frog-like cheeks? His tilted bell on his horn? His African robes later in life? His pointedly supercilious vocabulary? His outrageous twists and turns, with his deeply serious playing on frivolous tunes and his humor on serious ones? What was he telling the audience? And just which audience was he addressing?

The following vignette displays most of the characteristics I have discussed.

One night in Texas in the mid-1950s (Kliment 1988:75-76), the incomparable Ella Fitzgerald was sitting backstage eating a sandwich and watching the band members playing dice, a group that included renowned trumpeter Dizzy Gillespie. Fitzgerald was terrified by the sudden arrival of local law officials, who arrested the entire group for gambling. The officers, upset because the group was performing in an all-white theater, took them to the police station where they were booked and jailed—Fitzgerald still in her ball gown. During the booking process, an officer asked Gillespie for his name. He replied, "Louis Armstrong."

And that is what the officer wrote down. Several hours later, after the band's white manager paid the $50 bail, an arresting officer asked Ella Fitzgerald for her *autograph*. The next day, local papers reported that she was the best-dressed prisoner the jail ever held. (Iris Carter Ford: 43).

Giving his name as Louis Armstrong was humor, with many meanings within meanings. On one level it was humorous that the police did not recognize either Dizzy for who he was, but obviously recognized Ella for a famous vocalist. Dizzy was quite famous, and recognizable even to non-jazz fans. It was also an inside joke to pass himself off as Armstrong, whom most people would recognize at the time. Additionally, it was both a claim to be related in jazz to Louis, but also to show that their earlier feud had ended in a close and enduring friendship. Indeed, on hearing of Louis Armstrong's death Gillespie said "No him, no me," neatly summing up the history of jazz humor as well as jazz trumpet.

Laughin' Louie

There are a number of jokes on the record "Laughin' Louie". The first joke is the fact that Armstrong always referred to himself as "Lewis". He joked that white folks always pronounced his name as "Louie". In fact, on one poster his name is wrongly spelled "Lewis", obviously following his own pronunciation. So, it is not a far stretch to see the title as Armstrong laughing at those who think they are superior but cannot even pronounce his name correctly.

What else is Louis laughing at? Well, he is laughing at the fact that he and his Vipers recorded "Laughin' Louie" while high on marijuana. In 1931 Armstrong was high much of the time and "viper" was a slang expression for a pothead (Bergreen 1997:332, 360). The fact that he could use the expression for his band and even for his tune, "Song of the Vipers", was merely another in-joke on Satchmo's part at the expense of polite society. Additionally, to many people's amazement, Armstrong liked the Guy Lombardo big band sound. In 1931, Armstrong was fronting a "sweet" big band, one that featured whining saxophones as well as strict adherence to playing the melody the way it was written. At the same time, the band was reminiscent of Paul Whiteman's in including "hot" players. The mixture of Armstrong's melodic, but hot, trumpet over the sweet sound of the band is often funny. Whether Satchmo intended it to be humorous or not is arguable, but it has its unique charm and humor, in any case. It does contrast an overly up-tight style of music with a looser and even more sophisticated one.

Of course, the joke could just as well be on the hipster that put down Guy Lombardo's music. Armstrong, along with other jazz musicians, is an innate fusionist. They merge all sorts of music into jazz, adapting it to the idiom. Throughout his life, Armstrong flatly stated that he liked Lombardo's music. It is there in his music, just as Puccini's arias are there. The New Orleans tradition is a Creole one that delights in mixing categories in a rich gumbo. It is also clear that in this period Armstrong was reveling in black culture and eager to share it with his audience.

He included a great deal of inside jokes in his versions of popular songs. For example, his version of Hoagy Carmichael's "Old Rocking Chair" contains this response to Jack Teagarden's vocal statement that he is going to tan Louis's hide: "My hide's already tanned, Father!" Furthermore, Teagarden was white, a white trombonist who was slightly older than Armstrong and had early recognized his genius. The two had been close friends since the 1920s and cooperated in mocking racial stereotypes. The sly reference to miscegenation, a taboo subject in mixed company, slid by the censors. Armstrong gave white audiences a peak at black entertainment by performing vaudeville routines featuring a stock character, the corrupt Black Preacher, and many versions have been recorded. He referred often to his love for New Orleans food, early poverty, and details of black life. He turned them all into gentle jokes so that he could get on with his own love for life, and over his own pain.

The recording "Laughin' Louie" is filled with Armstrong's famous nonsense words, stammering, and bar after bar of laughter. Again, one asks what the joke is. Armstrong is Br'er Rabbit, again laughing at those who seek to best him. Armstrong was able to survive during the Depression when the market for "race records", those records aimed primarily at a black audience, had ended. He did so by following in the footsteps of other black performers, using race humor to his advantage. There is a long history of Africans and African Americans using humor to overcome hardships and to subvert ideas that endanger their survival. The use of humor, of course, offers a deniability of malice. The phrase "only kidding" was one that Armstrong often used. The article "African American Humor" in Alleen Pace Nilsen and Don L.F. Nilsen's Encyclopedia of the 20th Century American Humor (2000) offers numerous examples of this practice. The article, for instance, notes the similarity between west African humor and African American humor, noting the following common characteristics, characteristics already mentioned as prominent in Armstrong's stage style.

In west Africa, the original home of more than fifty per cent of American slaves, sociologists have found cultures with many of the same characteristics that African Americans rely on for their humor: extensive wordplay and punning, signifying (verbal put downs), the mocking of an enemy's relatives, the chanting and singing of ridicule verses, bent-knee dancing, an admiration for the trickster, and aggressive joking that demands verbal quickness and wit (Nilsen and Nilsen 2000:14). Salamone (1990), Keil (1979, 1992), and Crouch (2000), among others, have also noted similarities in the use of humor among Africans and African Americans, and in particular among African American and African musicians. Nilsen and Nilsen (2000) also note the popularity of black minstrelsy in the black community of the nineteenth century. Performers who mocked the old racial stereotypes by exaggerating them to their logical absurdities were also popular in the black community. Only later did white audiences become familiar with Moms Mabley and Pigmeat Markham, not to mention Redd Foxx. Armstrong used similar material in his own performances at a time when white audiences were familiar only with the comedy of Bert Williams, Eddie "Rochester" Anderson, and Stepin Fetchit.

Throughout his life, Armstrong collected jokes, copying them from joke books, newspapers, magazines, and friends. His archives at Queen's College are replete with his joke collection and jokes found in letters to friends. Many of these jokes refer to his color. For example, he refers to seeing Bojangles in the early 1920s. When the lights went out, Bojangles quipped, "Now the theater is my color." To Jon Hendricks's lyrics to Dave Brubeck's music for "In His Image God Made Man", Armstrong remarks, "Can God be black like me? My God!" It is a not-so-funny, funny moment. Satchmo delivers the line absolutely perfectly, reminding the listener of his version of Fats Waller's "Black and Blue".

Two of the jokes he saw fit to copy provide a glimpse into his humor. In a letter, Satchmo tells the one about the fly who walks on a mirror and says, "Well, that's another way to look at it." He also relates the story about the drunk and the ugly man. The drunk calls a man ugly in response to the man's taunt that he is drunk. The ugly man says, "Well, you are still drunk." The drunk has the last word and says, "Yeah, but in the morning you'll still be ugly!" [5]

Armstrong was always looking for another way to look at things in his music. He was aware that those who could not get past the color of a person's skin would still be ugly in the morning—it would be their own problem. He would go on with his life and laugh at what he could not change, for the most part. The haunting lines of Hendricks's lyric, "In His Image God Made Man", and Waller's "Black and Blue", reveal the pain out of which the humor emerged.

---

[5] This is usually attributed to Winston Churchill (but note the further attribution to WC Fields!): (From http://www.winstonchurchill.org/support/the-churchill-centre/publications/chartwell-bulletin/2011/31-jan/1052-drunk-and-ugly-the-rumor-mill):

The notion of him stumbling home drunk and wet, which I notice carries no attribution, is the invention of a fevered mind. It is a bowdlerization of an encounter between Churchill and a fellow Member of Parliament, related to me by the late Ronald Golding, the bodyguard present on that occasion:

Bessie Braddock MP: "Winston, you are drunk, and what's more you are disgustingly drunk."

WSC: "Bessie, my dear, you are ugly, and what's more, you are disgustingly ugly. But tomorrow I shall be sober and you will still be disgustingly ugly."

This world famous encounter occurred late one night in 1946, as Churchill was leaving the House of Commons. Lady Soames, who said her father was always gallant to ladies, doubted the story, but Mr. Golding explained that WSC was not drunk, just tired and unsteady, which perhaps caused him to fire the full arsenal.

Only later did I learn that he was probably relying on his photographic memory for this riposte: In the 1934 movie "It's a Gift", W.C. Fields's character, when told he is drunk, responds, "Yeah, and you're crazy. But I'll be sober tomorrow and you'll be crazy the rest of your life."

So the Bessie Braddock encounter was really Churchill editing W.C. Fields.

The Importance of Humor

Boskin (1986, 1997) and Burma (1946) note the function of humor in the subversion of ethnic stereotypes and as a means for carrying on verbal attacks on racism. There is little doubt that Armstrong used humor in such a manner, as many other African American comedians have done. That he was so adept at doing so through music is not surprising when placed in the African context. The African musicians Fela and Peter King, as well as the Gold Coasters, have brought that tradition into the modern world in Africa (Salamone 1990). It is a tradition also linked to calypso and other African-derived music (Manning 1983)—in short, it is a fundamental part of black humor and one that Armstrong employed throughout his career. Armstrong also tapped into another strong African tradition of humor, that of the trickster. Trickster, of course, appears in many traditions. The Navaho, for example, have many Coyote stories in which Coyote is the trickster. The Greeks had Hermes, from which we get the term for exegesis or explanation, "hermeneutics". However, it is the African Trickster who is most apropos to understanding Armstrong's humor.

In west African religions, the trickster is often a sacred character. Among the Yoruba of Nigeria, for instance, Eshu is a trickster who frequently disturbs the peace. He generally upsets the established order of things. However, the Yoruba view this upset as a good thing. Upsetting the established order keeps people on their toes and open to new ideas. Indeed, Trickster is the messenger of the gods and his disturbances are at divine behest, for they open the way to better communication through getting rid of obstacles and clearing away confusion. Eshu opens the path to new possibilities, and the Yoruba revere him as both a transformer and healer. African religion teaches that the fundamental order, which God has established, has as an integral part the paradox of constant change and subsequent renewal. Folktales have incorporated this concept through having a small but crafty animal use its cunning to defeat more powerful animals that seek to destroy it. Br'er Rabbit incorporates characteristics of many folk tricksters, including Anansi the spider from Ghana, Ajapa the Yoruba tortoise, and Sungura, a hare from the central and east African tradition (Ammons and White-Pak 1994, Pelton 1980, Smith 1994, and Hyde 1998.) It is not too far a stretch to note that Armstrong incorporated both folk and sacred functions in his art, just as other African musicians have long done (Salamone 1990). In fact, the Yoruba novelist Soyinka (1976) sees the genius of African artists lying in their use of mythic elements such as the trickster stories. Indeed, it is Trickster who is the very archetype of the artist, a position with which Hyde (1998) agrees. He also views the trickster as the archetypal form of the artist. After all, Trickster represents the power of the imagination. Though trickster culture reveals just how powerful the imagination, and by extension the artist, is in reshaping culture itself. Armstrong in a broader context.

Louis Armstrong was the first great soloist in jazz, with apologies to the outstanding Sidney Bechet, and turned jazz into a predominantly soloist's art (Collier 1983:160). Of course, his great sense of melodic form played a major role in his success, for arguably no jazz musician has ever constructed more perfectly structured melodic solos. But it is equally doubtful whether that sense of melody alone would have proved sufficient to usher in a new era of jazz. In addition to reworking melodies, Armstrong increased the feel for cross-rhythms in jazz. His improvisations ran the full gamut of the African characteristics in jazz: pitch, timbre, falsetto leaps, melismatic vocalizations, terminal vibratos, and, above all, adaptations of African cross-rhythms. As Miles Davis, an innovator in his own right, put it: "There is nothing done today on trumpet that does not owe a debt of gratitude to something Armstrong did first."[6] Without denying Armstrong's personal charisma, it is essential to ask what the relationship between his art and the times was. Why did jazz change from a group art to essentially a solo art form just when it did? When jazz began, somewhere around the turn of the century, it did so in reaction to the imposition of Jim Crow laws in New Orleans, a town that had been relatively open racially and had followed unprecedented social and cultural intercourse between the races. Jim Crow not only tended to segregate black and white, it also forced conservative Creoles into contact with those poor "street" blacks whom they had looked down upon (Jones 1967). The group improvisation of early New Orleans jazz can be viewed as a means for stating the need for racial unity among African Americans at a time of great sociocultural threat. Without stretching the point too much, it was music of solidarity in which each performer supported the others while staying out of their way.

Armstrong, moreover, tended to take a trickster's stance to American pop material. He tended to undermine it through seeming to embrace it. Armstrong reworked the material, putting his own variations on the theme, frequently transforming banal ditties into works of beauty. His music illustrates the entire approach-withdrawal dialectic of jazz. It exemplifies the ambivalent position of African Americans within American culture, for whenever Armstrong played anything, that piece was no longer ever heard

---

[6] This generally known by jazz fans: "You can't play anything on a horn that Louis hasn't played" (Miles Davis http://www.satchmo.com/louisarmstrong/quotes.html).

in quite the same way again. He managed to force people to look at the familiar in a new fashion, the way that he as an African American looked at it. Balliett (1994:73) notes that Armstrong was not a servile person.

Armstrong on stage was the same as Armstrong off stage—a tough, primitive, funny genius, full of high jinx and body jokes. He was also his own kind of racial activist: angrily quitting a State Department tour when Governor Faubus obstructed school integration in Arkansas. He made it possible for other soloists to tell their own stories, thereby increasing the value of the individual tale in a democratic society. Without Armstrong's rhythmic lesson, moreover, it is difficult to envision the emergence of the big band in jazz. Before his innovations, big bands tended to clunk along. They tended to apply European music's syncopation to jazz. Since jazz swing is not the result of syncopation as understood in European music, to jazz lovers the results tended to sound dreadful. Armstrong freed the soloist from the ground beat and moved jazz towards a more African approach to rhythm; namely, cross-rhythms, the presence of a number of rhythms that "cross" each other while not, ideally, getting in one another's way. True jazz swing is light, not ponderous, and it occurs on the on-, or up- beat.

Reflections on the Trickster

The fool appears to share the trickster's role as boundary-crosser, or as Karl Kerenyi put it, *"the enemy of boundaries"* (185). For the fool, as for the trickster, boundaries are not so much nonexistent as arbitrary (new or different boundaries can be created at will), and the comic play of his folly lies in his refusal to accept or recognize what seems self-evident to those who govern boundaries. In his negotiations with both sides of an arbitrary boundary, the fool enacts Mercurius's role as the "magical 'go-between'" (Nicholl 47), mediating between celestial and material, and thus comes closest to the key function of the trickster.

The difference is that the fool is playing, albeit playing "seriously" in the sense of total absorption in the role—"The contrast between play and seriousness is always fluid", says Johan Huizinga in *Homo Ludens* (1944), but play is not serious in the sense that it intends to produce results in the world beyond the game: "[i]t is rather a stepping-out of 'real' life into a temporary sphere of activity with a disposition all of its own" (8). The jester who baits the king, the fool crowned as "Lord of Misrule", observes strictly demarcated guidelines that confine their comic play to its own sphere, contained within the status quo. As another scholar of fools and clowns, Enid Welsford, has said, "There is nothing essentially immoral or blasphemous or rebellious about clownage. On the contrary, it may easily act as a social preservative by providing a corrective to the pretentious vanity of officialdom, a safety-valve for unruliness" (321). The fool, fundamentally, belongs to the world of orthodoxy, his comic play acting as a lubricant of the status quo. (Helen Lock, 'Transformations of the Trickster' (2002) 18 *Southern Cross Review*, available online at http://www.southerncrossreview.org/18/trickster.htm). As Jung also points out, the trickster's chaotic, accident-prone unconsciousness is not merely destructive, he is also creator and artist, miraculously salvaging order from mess and disaster, as Helen Lock has noted recently, following the work of Lewis Hyde.

In all this, "Trickster is the mythic embodiment of ambiguity and ambivalence, doubleness and duplicity, contradiction and paradox", and can thus be seen as the archetypal boundary crosser, although here Hyde notes that "there are also cases in which Trickster creates a boundary, or brings to the surface a distinction previously hidden from sight" (Preposterous trickster: myth, news, the law and John Marsden Marcus O'Donnell 282-305 Media Arts and Law Review 8, 2003): the fool, then, appears to share the trickster's role as boundary-crosser, or as Karl Kerenyi puts it, "*the enemy of boundaries*" (185). For the fool, as for the trickster, boundaries are not so much nonexistent as arbitrary (new or different boundaries can be created at will), and the comic play of his folly lies in his refusal to accept or recognize what seems self-evident to those who govern boundaries. In his negotiations with both sides of an arbitrary boundary, the fool enacts Mercurius's role as the "magical 'go-between'" (Nicholl 47), mediating between celestial and material, and thus comes closest to the key function of the trickster. The difference is that the fool is playing, albeit playing "seriously" in the sense of total absorption in the role—"The contrast between play and seriousness is always fluid", says Johan Huizinga in *Homo Ludens* (1944), but play is not serious in the sense that it intends to produce results in the world beyond the game; "[i]t is rather a stepping-out of 'real' life into a temporary sphere of activity with a disposition all of its own" (8). The jester who baits the king, the fool crowned as "Lord of Misrule", observe strictly demarcated guidelines that confine their comic play to its own sphere, contained within the status quo. As another scholar of fools and clowns, Enid Welsford, has said, "There is nothing essentially immoral or blasphemous or rebellious about clownage. On the contrary, it may easily act as a social preservative by providing a corrective to the pretentious vanity of officialdom, a safety-valve for unruliness" (321). "The fool, fundamentally, belongs to the world of orthodoxy, his comic play acting as a lubricant of the status quo".[7]

Reflections

The Eshu trickster from the Yoruba of Nigeria is a character who disturbs the peace by questioning norms and calling his people to be attentive skeptics of order. He also employs a crafty and cunning wit in the face of the more powerful, preserving his and others' freedom where it might potentially be curtailed. The Yoruba also parallel their trickster to the artist, celebrating his imaginative capacities and malleable skills. In all of these respects, Louis Armstrong may be regarded as a quintessential trickster, part of a long legacy passed from Africa and through slaveholding and segregated America.

In a broader context, Armstrong's trickster role can be tied to the jazz musical genre that he so transformed. Both were subject to—and responded to—unavoidable social realities, expressing pain and anger in reaction to a debilitating racism. Both also employed secret musical codes, employing protective masks that gave space to individual freedom and collective empowerment. Furthermore, both recognized humor as the license that permitted their liberationist expressions of thinly veiled social commentary. Jazz, like Armstrong, offered a language, the subtleties of which spoke to the in-crowd (the "hip") and about the outsiders (the "squares"). Invariably, it would privately mock either or both.

I mentioned Louis Armstrong's use of the trickster image in his rendition of "Laughin' Louie". Firstly, the "squares" are outed in the title itself, which parodies the common misinterpretation of his name in mainstream culture and mocks the one-dimensional stereotype with which he was regarded (and sometimes dismissed). From Armstrong's point-of-view, the title's humor might also allude to his habitual pot-smoking habits, this further underscored by the name of his accompanying band, the Vipers, a slang term for marijuana. The song's music fluctuates throughout, between the "hot" sound "hip" critics encouraged from Armstrong, and the "sweet" sounds he always had such affection for, but for which he was criticized as compromising to mainstream tastes. Here, the trickster celebrates his own creative choices (laughing for himself), and satirically dismisses the imposing judgment of his critics (laughing at them). This is achieved through the humorous method of incongruity, the

---

[7] Helen Lock, "Transformations of the Trickster" (2002) 18 *Southern Cross Review*, available online at http://www.southerncrossreview.org/18/trickster.htm.

shock of the juxtaposed styles surprising listeners into recognition and appreciation while appealing to many different audiences.

In considering audiences we must take note of the fact that Gillespie, as Armstrong before him, addressed multiple audiences. Indeed he was also a member of multiple audiences. As an African American southern musician he was always aware of his membership in Afro-American culture, his acculturation into the dominant white culture, his being a leading founder of bop, his maleness and many other memberships. His intelligence shone through as he played with these identities in his performances, juggling one against others as the mood moved him. Things were rarely, if ever, this *or* that; as Robert Farris Thompson (1964) has noted about Creole culture, they were this *and* that, too. (See also Roger D. Abrahams, Nick Spitzer, John F. Szwed and Robert Farris Thompson. Blues for New Orleans: Mardi Gras and America's Creole Soul. Philadelphia: University of Pennsylvania Press, 2006).

Diz was a master of mixing things together that often did not go together. He took risks others hesitated in taking. But he made you love him as he did so by turning his critique into a humorous comment or making it so seemingly outrageous that he couldn't really be serious. Except that, of course, he was. There was also a love for that which was human. At the height of the civil rights movement, I saw Dizzy drinking with a southern soldier who thought he was complimenting Diz, but was actually condescending to him. I sat at the bar expecting Diz to explode. Instead, he accepted the proffered drink, listened to the young soldier, and then made some off-handed remark that had the soldier laughing. The two walked off arm in arm.

To me, this incident is illustrative of Dizzy's being able to occupy a number of cultures and identities simultaneously. He often understood exactly where others were coming from and found ways to be diplomatic while getting his point across. As with Armstrong, he found a way to live his life the way he wanted while also finding a way to criticize people in ways they first listened too because they were humorous. No surprise, then, that they both were superb Jazz Ambassadors, representing America, yes, but also the need for greater equality and democracy in America. They understood that while they had a dual heritage, that heritage was an overlapping one and could not be neatly segregated as others believed. They were this *and* that, too. Cultures and boundaries are crossed, the mark of the quintessential Trickster.

Conclusion

As professor Neil Leonard writes in his book *Jazz: Myth and Religion*:

> For all true believers jazz answered needs that traditional faith did not address. While the music had different meanings for different followers—black, white, male female, young, old, rich or poor, in various psychological states and social situations—for all devotees it provided some form of ecstasy or catharsis transcending the limitations, dreariness and desperation of ordinary existence. As earthy blues, exalted anthem, or something in between, jazz could energize the most jaded will. Jazz is an active agent, a powerful force whose ecstasies, whether subtly insinuated or supplied in lightening illuminations, altered personality and society. Through cajolery, charm, warmth, surprise, shock or outrage it could brush aside the most entrenched tradition, the most oppressive custom, and inspire subversive social behavior. (Leonard, Neil. *Jazz: Myth and Religion*. Oxford University Press, 1987. pp. 1-2)

Leonard concludes:

> Consider how the jazzy music of the twenties went hand in hand with the upheavals in manners and morals of that time, how bop was the cry of street-wise young rebels in the forties, and how the "New Thing" of the sixties was closely allied to the "Black Power" impulse of the day. Clearly jazz is more than a passive flower, a glorious cultural ornament affirming humanity; it is also a powerful social force which has cut broadly and deeply, its prophets, rituals and myths touching not only individual souls but large groups bringing intimations of magic and the sacred to an era whose enormous changes have depleted conventional faiths.

In the hands of those who were more than mere masters, who possessed that certain something beyond mere excellence, call it charisma blended with a twinkle or personality—whatever one wishes to dub it, those trickster figures brought absolute joy to those whose lives they touched. When they entered a room, all eyes turned to them. They have the power to transform their surroundings. I felt that magic with the Bori doctor in the bush of northern Nigeria and I felt it in Armstrong's presence and in Dizzy's as well.

These men were transformative figures, beyond category in Duke Ellington's expression. They performed their alchemy not on base physical materials but rather they transformed artistic ones, taking music they found and turning it into high art. They took the everyday and turned it into something else. Leonard calls it religious. Charlie Parker, when asked what his religion was, said simply, "Jazz." Indeed, there is a Church of St.

John Coltrane in San Francisco on Fillmore Street (Church of St. John Coltrane African Orthodox Church (http://www.coltranechurch.org/). The music at the services there must be absolutely great!

References

Abdalla, Ismail H. (1991) Neither Friend nor Foe: The Malam Practitioner—yan bori relationship in Hausaland. IN I. M. Lewis, Ahmed Al-Safi, and Sayyid Hurreiz, Women's Medicine: The Zar-Bori Cult in Africa and Beyond. Edinburgh: Edinburgh University Press, pp. 37-48.

Arendt, H. (1955 & 1970) *Men in Dark Times,* London: Jonathan Cape

Badejo, Deidre. "The Yoruba and Afro-American Trickster: A Contextual Comparison." *Presence Africaine* 147 (1988):3-17.

Bakhtin, M. (1968) *Rabelais and His World,* Cambridge, Mass: Harvard University Press

Bayless, M. (1996) *Parody in the Middle Ages: The Latin Tradition,* Ann Arbour: University of Michigan Press

Benhabib, S. (1996) *The Reluctant Modernism of Hannah Arendt,* Thousand Oaks, Calif: Sage Publications

Besmer, Fremont E. Horses, Musicians & Gods The Hausa Cult of Possession-Trance (1983) Westport: Greenwood Publishing Group, Incorporated, Sept.

Blake, N., Smeyers, P. Smith, R., Standish, P. (1998) *Thinking Again: Education after Postmodernism,* London: Bergin and Garvey

Boston, R. (1974) *An Anatomy of Laughter,* London: Collins

Burke, P. (1992) *History and Social Theory,* Cambridge: CUP

Carr, W. and Hartnett, A. (1996) *Education and the Struggle for Democracy,* Buckingham: Open University Press.

Castoriadis, C. (1997), *World in Fragments: Writings on Politics, Society, Psychoanalysis and the Imagination,* Stanford, Stanford University Press.

Colley, L. (1992) *Britons: Forging the Nation 1707-1837* London: Vintage.

Conroy, J. (1999) 'Poetry and Human Growth', *Journal of Moral Education,* 28, 4, 491-510.

Cox, Harvey (1969) *The Feast of Fools: A theological essay on festivity and fantasy* Cambridge Mass: Harvard University Press

Davis, A. (1998) 'The Limits of Educational Assessment', *Journal of Philosophy of Education: Special Issue,* Vol. 32:1, March

Davis, Erick. Trickster at the Crossroads: West Africa's God of Messages, Sex and Deceit. http://www.techgnosis.com/chunkshow-single.php?chunk=chunkfrom-2005-06-15-2009-0.txt

Douglas, M. 'The Social Control of Cognition: Some Factors in Joke Perception', *Man* 3:361-376.

Echerd, Nicole (1991) Gender Relationships and Religion. Women in the Hausa Bori in Ader, Niger. In Catherine Coles and Beverly Mack, EDS. Hausa Women in the Twentieth Century. Madison: The University of Wisconsin Press, pp. 207-220.

—. (1991) The Hausa bori possession cult in the Ader region of Niger: Its origins and present-day Function. IN I. M. Lewis, Ahmed Al-Safi, and Sayyid Hurreiz, Women's Medicine: The Zar-Bori Cult in Africa and Beyond. Edinburgh: Edinburgh University Press, pp. 64-80.

Erasmus, Desiderius. *The Praise of Folly*. 1511. Trans. Hoyt Hopewell Hudson. Princeton, NJ: Princeton UP, 1941.

Erlmann, Veit (1982) Trance and Music. Ethno-musicology 26, 1:49-58.

Faulkingham, Ralph N. (1975) The Sprits and Their Cousins: Some Aspects of Belief, Ritual, and Social Organization in a Rural Hausa Village in Niger. Research Report Number 15. Department of Anthropology. University of Massachusetts, Amherst. October.

Ferguson, N. (2001) *The Cash Nexus: Money and Power in the Modern World 1700 – 2000*, Harmondsworth: Allen Lane The Penguin Press.

Foster, R. (1994) *Paddy and Mr Punch*, London: Verso

Francis, L. (2001) *The Values Debate- A Voice from the Pupils*, London: Woburn Press

Francis, L. Astley, J and Robbins, M. (2001) *The Fourth R for the Third Millennium: Education in Religion and Values for the Global Future*, Leamington spa: Lindisfarne

Gates, Henry Louis, Jr. *The Signifying Monkey: A Theory of African American Literary Criticism.* New York: OUP, 1988.

Gray, J. (1993 & 1996) *Post-Liberalism: studies in political thought*, London: Routledge.

Hamilton, Edith. *Mythology*. 1940. New York: Mentor, 1969.

Harrison, A. (1989) *The Irish Trickster*, Sheffield: Sheffield Academic Press.

Hay, D. (1968), *Europe: The Emergence of an Idea*, Edinburgh: Polygon.

Heaney, S. (1983) *Sweeney Astray*, London: Faber and Faber.

Helen Lock, 'Transformations of the Trickster'(2002) 18 *Southern Cross Review*, available online at

Howard, P.J and Howard, J. M. (2000) *The Big Five Quickstart: An Introduction to the Five-Factor Model of Personality for Human Resource Professionals* at http://www.centacs.com/quik-pt1.htm

Huizinga, Johan. *Homo Ludens: A Study of the Play-Element in Culture.* 1944. N.p.: Beacon, 1955.

Hyde, Lewis. *Trickster Makes This World: Mischief, Myth, and Art.* New York: Farrar, Strauss and Giroux, 1998.

Hynes, W. J. (1993) 'Inconclusive Conclusions: Tricksters: Metaplayers and Revellers' in Hynes, W. J. and Doty, W. G. *Mythical Trickster Figures*, Tuscaloosa & London: University of Alabama Press, 202-19.

Jackson, R. (1997) Religious education: An interpretative Approach, London: Hodder and Stoughton

Jarman, A. O. H. (1991) 'The Merlin Legend and the Welsh Tradition of Prophecy', in Bromwich, R. Jarman, A. O. H. and Roberts, Brynley F. (Ed) (1991) *The Arthur of the Welsh*, Cardiff: University of Wales Press, 117 – 147.

Jonson, B. (1962 & 1971) D.Cook (ed; Introduction and Notes) *Volpone*, London, Methuen

Jung, C.G. *Psychology and Alchemy.* 1944. Vol. 12 of *The Collected Works.* Trans. R.F.C. Hull. 2nd ed. Princeton, NJ: Princeton UP, 1968.

Jung, Carl "On the Psychology of the Trickster Figure." Collected Works Trans. R.F.C. Hull. Radin 195-211.1954-1966

Kabir, Zainab Sa'id. Triple Heritage: The Dilemma of the African Muslim Woman. HausaNet Article. www.hausanet.com/HausNet_Article_100115.htm

—. Triple Heritage: The Dilemma of the African Muslim Woman. HausaNet Article. WWW.hausanet.com/HausNet_Article_100115.htm

Kerenyi, Karl. "The Trickster in Relation to Greek Mythology. Pt. V: His Difference from Hermes." Trans. R.F.C. Hull. Radin 188-91.

Kingston, Maxine Hong. *Tripmaster Monkey: His Fake Book.* New York: Vintage, 1987.

Kuhn, T.S. (1970) *The Structure of Scientific Revolutions*, Chicago: University of Chicago, 2nd edn.

Last, Murray (1991) Spirit Possession as Therapy: Bori among non-Muslims in Nigeria. IN I. M. Lewis, Ahmed Al-Safi, and Sayyid Hurreiz, Women's Medicine: The Zar-Bori Cult in Africa and Beyond. Edinburgh: Edinburgh University Press, pp. 49-63.

Leonard, Neil *Jazz--Myth and Religion.* Oxford University Press, 1987

Lewis, I. M., Ahmed Al-Safi, and Sayyid Hurreiz (1991) Women's Medicine: The Zar-Bori Cult in Africa and Beyond. Edinburgh: Edinburgh University Press.

Lyotard, J-F. (1979) *La Condition postmoderne*, Paris: Minuit.
Frederick-Malanson, Linda. Three African Trickster Myths/Tales -- Primary Style. http://www.yale.edu/ynhti/curriculum/units/1998/2/98.02.04.x.html
Masquelier, Adeline (2001) Prayer Has Spoiled Everything: Possession, Power, and Identity in an Islamic Town in Niger. . Durham: Duke University Press.
McNally, D. (1993) *Against the Market: Political Economy, Market Socialism and the Marxist Critique*, London: Verso
Momaday, N. Scott. *House Made of Dawn.* New York: Harper, 1966.
Morrison, Toni. "Recitatif." *Confirmation.* Ed. Amiri and Amina Baraka. New York: Morrow, 1983. Rpt. in The Norton Anthology of American Literature. Vol. 2. 5th ed. Ed. Nina Baym et al. New York: Norton, 1998. 2077-92.
Muldoon, P. (1998) *Hay*, London: Faber and Faber.
Myers, I.B., & McCaulley, M.H. (1985). *Manual: A Guide to the Development and Use of the Myers-Briggs Type Indicator.* Palo Alto: Consulting Psychologists Press.
Na Gopaleen, M. (Flann O'Brien) (1968) *The Best of Myles*, (ed. K.O'Nolan) London: Picador
Nicholl, Charles. *The Chemical Theatre.* 1980. New York: Akadine, 1997.
Norman, W.T. (1963) 'Toward an adequate taxonomy of personality attributes: Replicated factor structure in peer nomination personality rating', *Journal of Abnormal and Social Psychology*, 66, 574-583.
O' Riain, P. (1972) 'A Study of the Irish Legend of the Wild Man', *Eigse*, xiv, 179-206.
Oppong, Christine, ed. (1983) Male and Female in West Africa. London: Allen and Unwin. (Includes Enid Schildkrout, "Dependence and Autonomy: The Economic Activities of Secluded Hausa Women in Kano"; Pittin, Renee, "Houses of Women: A Focus in Alternative Life-Styles in Katsina City")
Parekh, B. (2001) *Rethinking Multiculturalism: Cultural Diversity and Political Theory*, London: Macmillan.
Pelton, Robert D. *The Trickster in West Africa: A Study of Mythic Irony and Sacred Delight.* Berkeley: U of California P, 1980.
Pittin, Renee. (1979). Marriage and Alternative Strategies: Career Patterns of Hausa Women in Katsina City. Ph.D. diss., School of Oriental and African Studies, University of London.
Pittock, Murray G. H. (1999) *Celtic Identity and the British Image*, Manchester: Manchester University Press.
Pluralism, Africa, 45, 1975, pp.401-424.

Radin, Paul. *The Trickster: A Study in American Indian Mythology.* 1956. New York: Schecken, 1971.
Rest, J., Narvaez. D., Bebeau, M.J. and Thomas, S. (1999) *Postconventional Moral Thinking*, N.Y: Lawrence Erlbaum.
Rorty, R. (1999) *Philosophy and Social Hope*, London: Penguin.
Salamone, Frank A. (1975). Becoming Hausa - Contributions to a Theory of Cultural
—. (1977). Religion as Play: Bori – A Friendly "Witchdoctor." In David Lancy and B. Allan Tindall, EDS. The Study of Play: Problems and Prospects. West Point, NY: Leisure Press, pp. 158-167.
—. The Culture of Jazz: Jazz as Critical Culture; Lanham: University Press of America, 2008.
Smith, Jeanne Rosier. *Writing Tricksters: Mythic Gambols in American Ethnic Literature.* Berkeley: U of California P, 1997.
The Church of St. John Coltrane. African Orthodox Church. Accessed February 12, 2013.http://www.coltranechurch.org/
Turner, V. (1969) *The Ritual Process: Structure and Anti-Structure,* Chicago: Aldine
Ugorji, Okechukwu K. *The Adventures of Torti: Tales from West Africa.* Trenton, NJ: African World Press, 1991.
Vizenor, Gerald. *Darkness in Saint Louis Bearheart.* St. Paul: Truck P, 1978
—. *The Heirship Chronicles.* Minneapolis: U of Minnesota P, 1990.
Welsford, E. (1935) *The Fool: His Social and Literary History,* London: Faber and Faber.
Welsford, Enid. *The Fool: His Social and Literary History.* 1935. Gloucester, MA: Peter Smith, 1966.

CHAPTER THREE

JAZZ IN ROCHESTER IN THE CONTEXT OF THE WIDER SCENE

The founders of the Umbria Jazz Festival are fond of citing a New York Times article of a few years ago stating that Umbria had developed a new type of jazz, jazz Italian-style. The founders point out that this is nothing new, for some of the early founders of jazz were Italian Americans like Nick LaRocca and Joe Venuti. They could have added Eddie Lang and many others who played with the best African American musicians of the day. I broached this point some years ago with Gap (Gaspare) Mangione, the elder of the Mangione Brothers. Chuck is the younger brother. Gap agreed that there is a difference in "Italian" jazz. It is, he stated, a subgenre of jazz, something generally more melodic.

Jazz in Rochester, NY, developed within the larger framework of jazz in the United States. Within that larger scene, Italians played a significant role, along with, of course, African Americans, and people of many other cultures. The fact that there are subgenres of jazz is evidence of the very democratic nature of the music itself. It is able to assimilate different elements and styles from different ethnic groups, social classes, and religions and yet maintain its identity in the midst of change. The ever-evolving art that is jazz is capable of fusing various elements into the whole while respecting the uniqueness of each group that contributes to the mix. Enrico Rava, an outstanding Italian jazz trumpet player, notes that you can generally tell an Italian musician from a German, but both are playing jazz. It is part of the democratic genius of jazz that it is able to live up to the motto of the United States, *E Pluribus Unum* (Out of Many, One).

Early Jazz

The traditional story of jazz tends to follow a trajectory leading from west Africa via the West Indies to New Orleans. En route, African Americans, usually enslaved, merged African rhythms with European harmonies. Et voilà, jazz was born! The only role for any whites in this tale is that of exploiters who stole the creation of blacks, watered it down, commercialized it and profited from this ersatz creation.

Recent scholarship, however, has questioned this overly simplistic view of the development of the art form. Certainly, there is no doubt that African Americans were, and have remained, its outstanding practitioners. However, there is also little doubt that others have also contributed to its creation and development. Kevin Whitehead (2000), for example, argues for a more complex understanding of the evolution of the art form. In discussing the international flavor of jazz, Whitehead notes a couple who took the boat to New Orleans and had a son who grew up to be Original Dixieland Jazz Band cornetist Nick LaRocca. All those Italians in old New Orleans were one reason opera was in the air, helping inspire Louis Armstrong's dramatic high-note endings.

Nick LaRocca, Eddie Lang and Joe Venuti were major contributors to the development of early jazz. In reviewing "The Creation of Jazz: Music, Race, and Culture in Urban America", Joyner notes that there has been a marked increase in interest in the sociocultural aspects of jazz history. Paretti has noted major social themes related to jazz

The main social themes are already well known topics in jazz studies: (1) jazz was a major vehicle for African American achievement and social recognition; (2) it also served as a vehicle for cultural liberation of young white musicians; (3) it was nurtured by urbanization and disseminated by the black Diaspora as well as mass media technology; and (4) gender roles have been as integral as racial roles to the character of jazz. (Paretti 1994:4). Point 3 is important to understanding the involvement of Italian Americans in jazz.

As Joyner comments, Paretti observes that whites in New Orleans were not attempting to imitate black musicians; they were convinced that whites had invented jazz. He notes that the members of the white band the New Orleans Rhythm Kings did not agree with this. Paretti does hold that many Italians found a release in jazz and musicians, such as Louis Prima, revered black culture.

Dominick James (Nick) LaRocca was a leader and trumpet player of the Original Dixieland Jazz Band, or, as the band originally spelled it, Jass Band. The ODJB was from New Orleans and recorded the first jazz record in 1917, "Livery Stable Blues", when Freddy Keppard refused to do so. Far from being a watered down joke, the ODJB paved the way for other groups to spread the jazz gospel. Louis Armstrong praised LaRocca, naming his as a pioneer of jazz.

In addition to Nick LaRocca, there were many other New Orleans Italian American musicians. Leon Rappolo, also of the ODJB, recorded with Jelly Roll Morton, the self-proclaimed creator of jazz. Indeed, New Orleans had a long tradition of "mixed bands". In pre-segregation New Orleans, for example, Jack Laine had three African Americans, two Italian Americans, two Mexicans, an Irish American, a Filipino and a German. The point is that many different groups, including Italian Americans, had some part in the gumbo that became jazz.

Quite soon, certainly by 1917 when the ODJB went to New York, jazz spread to many other areas of the country. Italian American musicians were quick to join the ranks of the new music. Among the more innovative of these musicians were Eddie Lang (Salvatore Massaro) and Joe Venuti from Philadelphia. Lang, who like so many musicians had a father who was a musician, learned to play guitar from his own father. Lang became known as the Father of Jazz guitar, performing with many of the leading jazz artists of his time. He and Joe Venuti, a violinist, often teamed up.

Lang, however, was the more innovative and influential of the two. His work became the pattern for future jazz guitarists. I became aware of Lang, whose work I had known marginally, when interviewing a young guitarist, Larry Luger, who is an American of German and Italian ancestry. Luger urged me to listen carefully to Lang, who still inspires and awes young guitarists. Lang became the first famous jazz guitarist, playing with the likes of Bix Beiderbecke, The Mound City Blue Blowers, Louis Armstrong, King Oliver, Paul Whiteman, and others.

Venuti's career was a long one; he first recorded with Eddie Lang in 1927. Along the way, Venuti established himself as an important musician as well as a practical joker. He loved to entertain, following a long tradition of Italian musicianship, and continued to be active in music until his death in 1978. His last recording was with Joe Romano: it highlights his humor as well as his ability. On "Angelina", Venuti and Romano decide to sing, but in a Yiddish accent. However, before and after the humorous vocal, Venuti displays a beautiful tone and deep respect for the melody.

In The Treasured Traditions of Louisiana Music (www.louisianafolklife.org), Ben Sandmel points out the Creole nature of New Orleans music in general. It is a place where traditions are blended into ever-changing new combinations. Sandmel notes that immigrants have always brought their music to Louisiana and blended it with what was already there. Among these traditions, he says, was "Italian music, and its fascinating interaction with jazz and rhythm & blues".

Certainly, Italians and Italian American in New Orleans and other centers of early jazz played a significant role in the creation and spread of early jazz. Certainly, the earliest of the great musicians and audiences may have been black. However, many Italians were living in the back of town neighborhoods, as Armstrong himself notes. Italians and Jews joined these musicians in playing, because in the earliest days of jazz no one knew the music *was* jazz. There was a long history of white and black playing together in New Orleans.

Moreover, unlike blues, jazz is not a folk music. It has had a strong European component from its earliest days. Its originators could and did read music; many Creoles and Italian musicians were trained in European classical music. Those who were self-trained generally learned to read music, and read it well. Louis Armstrong, for example, eventually read music quite well, and spoke of his love for Italian opera and Jewish Russian lullabies. To hone his reading abilities he played in a pit band in Chicago during the day and received ovations for his solos on European masterpieces, including Italian compositions (cf Louis Armstrong, In His Own Words, 2001).

Enrico Rava

On January 15, 2004, I interviewed Enrico Rava, an Italian trumpet player, who was in New York as part of the promotion for the Umbria Jazz Festival. I decided to test my ideas regarding Italian jazz on him. I asked him whether there were any differences between Italian jazz and other forms of jazz. He had obviously given serious thought to the question on his own, for he responded very quickly and with great clarity. In essence, he stated that jazz is jazz; it is a unity.

However, he went on, there are certain characteristics found in jazz played by Italians or Italian Americans. Among these characteristics, he believed, were the depth of emotion and singing quality of the music. There is a strong melodic element in the music of those sharing an Italian heritage, coming, Rava believes, from exposure to operatic arias and Neapolitan music. He concludes that in general the way Italians play jazz is different from the way others do. He spoke about the Mangione brothers as examples, among many others, of what he was meant. Even when he played atonal and free jazz, he was fond of searching for the melodic elements buried in these forms.

Not surprisingly, he names Louis Armstrong, Bix Beiderbecke and Miles Davis as his major influences—all known for their melodic playing and technique. It was after he met Miles that he bought his first trumpet.

He had been listening to Bix, whose picture was on his wall from when he was ten years old. Rava was eighteen when Miles came to his hometown and befriended him—within two years, Rava had left home.

It is interesting that although Rava is a modern player, influenced by Dizzy Gillespie and Clifford Brown, he states that he still listens to Louis Armstrong every day. It reminds one of Miles Davis's statement that there is nothing played on the trumpet that Armstrong did not play first. Dizzy also said it simply, "No him, no me." Rava said that Armstrong's music was "one of the ten things that makes life worth living. The beauty of his playing is one of life's blessings". "Even when Italy was in what we might call a primitive state," Rava said, "people knew Armstrong and related to his music because of its beauty." Rava, who for many years was known as a "free" player, said he would choose beauty over style any day. He even ventured that today's jazz is less interesting than that of the past because there were so many geniuses in the past, including the underrated Pete LaRocca of the Original Dixieland Jazz Band. He was one of many Italian musicians who contributed to the overall mosaic of jazz, borrowing and adding to its complexity.

Some Italians in Jazz History

The list of Italians in jazz history is a long one. Simply listing the major figures is intimidating. There have been many formidable creative Italian artists in jazz. A brief list gives the idea of their significance. Among the many great figures in jazz are these Italian Americans: Sam Noto, Flip Phillips, Bucky Pizzarelli, Charlie Ventura, Armando Anthony (Chick) Corea, Buddy de Franco, Carl Fontana, Buddy Greco, Johnny Guarnieri, Nick LaRocca, Eddie Lang, Henry Mancini, Chuck Mangione, Gap Mangione, Joe Marsalis, Pat Martino, Joe Morello, Vido Musso, Sammy Nestico, Sal Nistico, Al Dimeola., Joe Lavano, Joe Romano, and Louis Prima.

This brief sample provides some idea of the role that Italian Americans have played in jazz. Although many different styles of jazz are represented—from early New Orleans to avant-garde—there are found the characteristics that Rava noted in our interview, namely, a singing quality in the playing and a love for melody. Almost inevitably, when given a choice of notes to play in their improvisations, these musicians tend to choose the "pretty" note. It is an interesting characteristic, one that Gap Mangione also noted in our interview (July 5, 1989). He stated, "There was a thriving, informal, let's-play-together kind of scene going." He noted a number of players from the western New York area who went on to fame: "I can remember people like Sam Noto, Larry Cavelli, Don Menza, coming from Buffalo—Sal Nistico from Syracuse—Roy McCurdy, and Ron Carter, and Steve Gadd and Joe Romano and great players here. There was a conglomeration of great players around that I remember."

I noticed the melodic characteristic, which Mangione mentions, on June 28, 2005 while attending a jazz performance in White Plains, New York. The Jazz Forum All Stars were playing. Led by Mark Morganelli, the All Stars comprise four Italian American musicians. Each is a seasoned veteran of the New York metropolitan area jazz scene. Each has impressive jazz credentials and has performed with famous musicians. The setting was an outdoor courtyard with fountains. The weather was humid and warm.

The musicians, dressed in neat casuals, responded to every bit of applause and even body language of members of the audience. There was a bit of conversation, gracious response to requests and no show of petulance at being interrupted. It was a professional-friendly wooing of those who came to spend some time. This wooing extended to the repertoire.

Most of the material came from the Great American Songbook, familiar pop songs. Bossa Nova also made up its share of the choices. In addition, there was a Miles Davis tribute and some jazz standards. Morganelli made sure he explained the jazz standards, providing a biography, for example of Clifford Brown, his early death in an automobile accident at 26, and his influence to the present. All this was done without any condescension to those in the audience who have limited, if any, knowledge of jazz and with an eye to winning over youngsters in the audience.

Consciously, I took note of just how often the musicians chose the "pretty" note when give a choice and constructed new beautiful melodies on top of the originals. Jay Azzolina, for example, a guitarist who has played with Chuck Mangione, Harvie S, Spyro Gyra, John Pattituci, Pat Methany, and others, constantly surprised the audience with fully developed counter-melodies on top of familiar tunes such as "The Girl from Ipanema", or "All the Things You Are". Rick Petrone, a bassist who has played with Marian McPartland, Buddy Rich, Chet Baker, the Thad Jones-Mel Lewis Band, Mel Torme, and others, not only kept the rhythm but also supplied melodic, coherent, and supportive solos. Joe Coscello, the drummer, has played with Zoot Simms, John Bunch, Gene Bertoncini, Barry Miles, Jack Wilkins, Don Elliott, Sal Salvadore, Marian McPartland, Benny Goodman, Joe Venuti, Red Norvo, Milt Hinton, Peggy Lee and

Tony Bennett, among others. Joe's noted brush work was on display. He kept out of the way of soloists, added to the ensemble, and when given the opportunity soloed tastefully. The entire experience was one of immersing oneself into the familiar, with surprises popping up, and the beautiful.

The concert summed up the Italian American jazz ethos. Morganelli's group wooed the audience, communicating it while watching their responses to what it did. There was a conscious effort to create something beautiful while moving into new avenues, creating new melodies or interesting rhythmic patterns. The familiar was used to lead people to the unfamiliar. There appeared to be a conscious effort to delve into the inner workings of the melody to find hidden elements there. There was a clear connection between melody and harmony. Rather than limiting creativity, this approach seemed to unleash it, finding outlets for formidable technique in the service of "singing" the song. Rather than a string of notes or squeals, there is an attempt to add to the beauty and truth of the tune.

Louis Prima

In many ways, Louis Prima was the quintessential Italian musician of his time. He was outgoing, funny, and wanted to win his audience over. His nickname was "The Italian Satchmo", and Prima acknowledged his debt to Louis Armstrong. Like Armstrong, he had to face criticism because of his popularity and willingness to entertain as well as play jazz. His big band's motto was "Play Pretty for the People".

Prima was able to play "serious" jazz because he entertained the public. His career extended over more than forty years. He managed to keep the essence of swing and Dixie while changing with the times. Like Armstrong, he enjoyed the music of Guy Lombardo, a taste most jazz fans found incredible. He was, in fact, Lombardo's protégé. This openness helped perpetuate his career. Prima began to bring some hints of Rock music into his playing, with the help of the underrated Sam Buttera. The use of vaudeville routines, along with Keely Smith, for example, also seduced an audience that might not otherwise go to hear a jazz musician.

It needs to be remembered that Prima, like Armstrong and many jazz musicians was from New Orleans. Prima left New Orleans to open at the Famous Door in New York City. Moreover, Prima was one of many New Orleans Italian American musicians who throughout their careers continued to perform and hang out with black musicians. Additionally, these musicians openly admitted their debt to black musicians. Often, Prima and others were advocates of racial equality.

Even though the 1900s was hardly a time of enlightened racial attitude and the South was a very unlikely place for racial progress, it was, nonetheless, in New Orleans that, at the turn of the century, a symbolic racial epoch was created. Here, within the confines of "making music", whites and blacks for the first time came to appreciate one another's talent, creative output, and individual personality traits.

This epoch did not, of course, foster a larger movement toward racial understanding and legal equality. However, it did, albeit on a limited basis, give whites an opportunity to observe racial discrimination from the "black's perspective". Because white musicians emulated black musicians, they followed them to the clubs or private parties where they might be performing. Here they would see how blacks would be engaged to entertain the white guests, but forbidden to mingle, drink, or eat with them; allowed to perform what was derisively called "bawdyhouse music", but prohibited from letting a white musician join them onstage (Bourland: The Journal of Ethnic Studies 16:1:53).

Prima was, interestingly, a favorite with black audiences. Many people, including promoters, believed him to be black because of his skin color. Prima also used many black performers in his group and performed at the Apollo and other black venues. His openness cost him jobs as bigoted New York promoters refused to hire him, ostensibly because they thought he was African American. Nonetheless, Prima continued to defy the segregationist policies of the country as Gary Bourland notes (The Journal of Ethnic Studies 16:1).

Prima tended to ignore restrictions that got in the way of his performance. He performed with Teddy Wilson and Lionel Hampton, and Art Tatum was Prima's opening act at the Famous Door in 1937. Prima was the only white bandleader in the 1930s and 1940s who performed at the leading black theaters of the day, the Howard in Washington and the Apollo in New York. Prima was not only steeped in the tradition of New Orleans greats, but was a fine entertainer as well.

These efforts were noted by no less than Eleanor Roosevelt. As Bourland notes:

> By 1941, the First Lady had become a vocal advocate of ripping down the walls of segregation, arguing that the prevalence of tuberculosis and rising crime were attributable not just to lack of education and to physical differences, but are due in large part to the basic fact of segregation which we have set up in this country and which warps and twists the lives not only of our Negro population, but sometimes of foreign born or even religious groups (Bourland).

Times change, and although Prima continued to work for integration in his way, that way was looked down on in the 1960s. Prima did not sign Civil Rights statements, as did Marlon Brando, for example. He did not march in parades. He did continue to protest segregation in Las Vegas and resist efforts to get him to stop socializing with performers such as Cab Calloway. What did not change with Prima was his desire to please his audience and incorporate elements of music that would enable him to do so.

Rochester, NY, in the Broader Context

From the earliest days of the twentieth century, Rochester had a lively music scene. Italians there had a love for music, and every festivity had its own music. The typical two-day wedding feasts required live musicians to keep the dancing and party going. In common with Italians elsewhere, many of Rochester's Italians were attracted to jazz, and as jazz became a popular music, performed it well. There was great pride in Italians who succeeded in any field of endeavor, and I recall how Louis Prima drew large crowds in Rochester. Entire families went to see the man who would "play pretty for the people".

Rochester was on various entertainment circuits. In the 1950s, for example, it was on the Birdland circuit. My father took me to see Charlie Ventura at a club when I was just a bit too young to meet the then legal age of 18 for entry. Charlie came over and sat with us at the bar. He found a way to communicate with a working man the intricacies of music, while winking at me. He said he often worked into his performance any request, even if it was just for a bar or two. This desire to impress the audience, while not unique to Italians, is part of the general culture, certainly of the culture of performance.

The 1950s were particularly rich times. As one participant, Noal Cohen puts it:

> Since the Eastman School of Music was located in Rochester, the local scene was substantially enriched by many talented Eastman students interested in jazz, even though no jazz studies program existed then. Nonetheless, I can well remember jam sessions held in the tiny Eastman practice rooms with a dozen or so musicians packed in so tightly that there was barely enough air to breathe!

Thus the local scene, which already boasted such budding stars as the Mangione Brothers, bassist Frank Pullara, drummer Roy McCurdy, saxophonists Pee Wee Ellis, Benny Salzano and Joe Romano and others, was enhanced and fertilized by Eastman students including bassist Ron Carter, pianists Wolf Knittel and Paul Tardif, saxophonists Larry Combs and Al Regni, and trumpeter Waymon Reed. John Eckert, another fine trumpet player, was also part of this scene although, like myself, he was a student at the University of Rochester rather than at Eastman (Noal Cohen's Jazz History Website, http://www.attictoys.com/jazz/index.html).

There is still a family-like feeling among many of the musicians who came up in Rochester. Note the number of Italians, but not only Italians, who came up together and who had contact with the Mangione Brothers, Chuck and Gap. I wrote in a review of Gap's "Stolen Moments" CD: "A number of world-class musicians have come from Rochester, NY, and nearby towns. Many have passed through the Mangione sphere of influence. Many record with one or both brothers from time to time. Each brother loves to teach and promote fellow musicians... This family-like feeling is felt on 'Stolen Moments'. The musicians are familiar with each other's work".

However, as Cohen demonstrates on his excellent website, this closeness did not mean that they were insular or isolated. Many great people came through town. A number of them, in fact, found themselves accepting invitations to Mama and Papa Mangione's table for a spaghetti dinner. Cohen presents a number of tables showing advertised jazz concerts in Rochester.

Frequently, the famous musicians invited local players to join them on the stand. Oscar Peterson did so in a famous jam session, as did Dizzy Gillespie on numerous occasions. Cohen has a picture on his site of Peterson's jam in which local musicians joined his trio in performance. His caption reads, "Oscar Peterson with some young Rochester musicians at a jam session held at The University of Rochester, Rochester, NY, 1957. Left to right: Noal Cohen, drums; Chuck Mangione, trumpet; Ron Carter, bass; Waymon Reed, trumpet; Benny Salzano, tenor saxophone; Oscar Peterson, piano" (Cohen http://www.attictoys.com/jazz/OPJam.html).

Gap Mangione shared a memory with me:

> ...about the time when I was still young enough, I had a driver's license but didn't have a car. I had a girlfriend who did have a car. It was a little Renault with a 5-speed transmission. Of course, at the time, those were very unusual. I had such a great time driving it that we tried to find reasons to go and drive somewhere. We heard there was a group playing over near Geneva. Geneva is a few miles south-east of Rochester, and it was kind of outside Geneva. Geneva is a small enough town, outside of Geneva is really the boondocks; this is the night before New Year's Eve about 1958, I think. So we drove down to the place where this jazz group was supposed

to be playing. Getting there was like small roads with ruts on either side. And finally, at the end of one road, there was a house, a large house that had the usual beer signs in the window. We went in and there was a fairly large, long bar and there were these people who were obviously workers. None of them were in suits, to put it delicately. And they were there for their after-work beer. And in the back, at the end of this bar was some room where they would normally serve sandwiches at noon time for people who might come by. And there was a band playing there, and I could see people dancing, but I couldn't believe the music I was hearing. So we went into the back room, and it was Philly Joe Jones, Paul Chambers, Sonny Clark, and Cannonball Adderley. On an off-night in December, there were maybe 30 or 40 people back there, some of them were dancing; that's how I met Cannonball Adderley, That night he asked my brother and I to play, and we did. I'm sure that you remember the reason we got the Jazz Brothers on record was because we were on the "Cannonball Adderley Presents" series on Riverside. About a year and a half later, we were playing in a club and I got a phone call there in the club from Cannonball asking if we'd be interested in recording for Riverside.

At that time, jazz musicians were, by and large, very eager to recruit youngsters into the profession. It was a time when jazz still appeared to be able to hold some of its own against the rock 'n' roll incursion. Italians made up a significant proportion of the overall musicians nationally. Rochester contributed many of its local players to that mix.

Conclusion

Scholarship in jazz history tends to be drawn along racial lines, with most historians in agreement that jazz was invented, nurtured, and defined by Afro-Americans, but assimilated and perhaps compromised in its creative integrity by whites. Such generally accepted equations overlook the integral ethnic role played by hundreds of Italian Americans who, during the first decades of this century, gave to jazz their own voice and, together with blacks of New Orleans, helped to export a raw, fresh and vital musical movement to the world. In retrospect, it should be no surprise that the Italian Americans of New Orleans played a substantive role in the formation of American jazz, even if one were to make a cursory study and look at demographics alone. In 1910, there were more Italian Americans in New Orleans than in any other city in the United States (Gary Bourland, The Journal of Ethnic Studies 16:1:52).

There has been a somewhat mild attempt to acknowledge the contributions of non-African Americans to the development of jazz. Bourland's significant article on Italian Americans in jazz is part of a larger body of work. The most comprehensive overall study is that of Richard M. Sudhalter's "Lost Chords: White Musicians and their Contribution to Jazz, 1915-1945". The book, by his admission, is a "vast and sprawling chronicle". One of its prescient conclusions is that "white musicians have been an integral force in jazz from its earliest days" (1999:744). Sudhalter argues cogently that in the early days of jazz there were important differences between the playing of black and white musicians based on social and cultural characteristics. The more similar the backgrounds of musicians, the more alike the styles and vice-versa. He cites Amiri Baraka's "Blues People" (1963:153) on this point. I would like to carry Sudhalter's point a bit farther. I believe that at least some of the differences may exist into the present, at least in subtle ways.

Certainly, Italian Americans were, and have continued to be, "an integral force in jazz". They have particular playing characteristics and preferences that have continued into the present. As Rava and Gap Mangione have noted, there is an almost inherent love for melody and harmony among Italian and Italian American musicians. Rava noted that even when playing atonal avant-garde music, other musicians in the group teased him about somehow finding a melodic line to play during his solos. He joked that some of his fellow musicians thought that he must be CIA because of his penchant for melody.

I do not wish to imply that all melodic music is at root Italian, nor that all Italian musicians at all times evince a love for melody in their performances. It would be an overgeneralization to say that a love for melody marks Italian and Italian American jazz musicians, or that a love for entertaining the audience is found in every such musician, but it would not be far from the truth. Those musicians who are not associated with melodic innovations, or who are somewhat shy on stage, are few, and even they can surprise. Briefly, I would mention Lennie Tristano and Chick Corea. Critics often cited Tristano's reluctance to play full-blooded tunes. His music was considered rather abstract and cold. However, there were exceptions that hint at greater depths.

Tristano recorded a significant work in 1949 that is now recognized as an early, if not the first, example of "free jazz". The two sides were "Intuition" and "Digression". There was no reference to time, tonality, or melody. Note that these experimental works were the result of Tristano's obsession with feeling and sincerity. Tristano became a major influence on Charles Mingus, who studied with him, as did Sal Mosca, Phil Woods, Lee Konitz and Warne Marsh. Note the regard for feeling and sincerity in his music. The recordings reflect a quiet beauty.

Corea is easier to tie into the tradition. His straight-ahead jazz performances and his classical ones demonstrate his clear mastery of melody. However, his Elektric Band may present problems to those who have a different view of melody from Corea. Corea has a very fresh outlook on music and the nature of æsthetics. He envisions melodies in many aspects of life and is often inspired by the wealth of beauty he finds in the world around him. He said: "The actual act of composing music is similar to the act of painting or writing a poem [in that] you summarize life [...] You see a nice sunset; you're the one whose mocking it up because you notice that it's beautiful. It's you that's imbuing it with beauty. And your next step would be a poem or a dance step or a melody" (http://www.imageandmusic.co.uk/corea.htm). Thus, even the often-shattering sound of his electronic music is meant to convey beauty, and Corea often surprises by breaking up his electric performances with very subtle melodies that are deeply moving. He even does some shy entertaining by a sudden widening of his grey eyes as he tossed his head up in mock surprise, adding an Italian shrug to the audience.

Ronald Morris notes, "The Sicilian approach to their peasant music offers five strong similarities to black music, sociologically if not clearly musically". Morris points to casinos where both blacks and Italians were in frequent attendance, black and Italian "itinerant musicians", parades, brass bands, and funerals, which were popular events with both groups, and finally a shared vision of what music represented: Sicilians were much like black people in seeing music as a highly personalized affair, a reflection of an individual's feelings, although born of a collective experience" (1980, p.840). These structural similarities supplemented cultural and emotional ones, leading to Italian contributions to America's greatest indigenous art form, jazz.

It is important to note that Chuck and Gap Mangione are Sicilians whose Sicilian father and mother invited numerous African American musicians to the home, including Sara Vaughan, Dizzy Gillespie, Jon Hendricks, and Cannonball Adderley, among others. Moreover, the rescue of an infant African-American child who was unable to breathe led to the family store's protection during the riots of the 1960s. In fact, Chuck sometimes had a bad rap from some white musicians because he played "too black".

Unfortunately, the contribution of Italian musicians to jazz, as well as that of other white musicians, is suffering under a Jim Crow mentality. As Terry Teachout (1995:50) writes, "Race-consciousness—on the part of individuals and institutions alike—is now a powerful force in the world of jazz, one whose effects have only just begun to come clear". There has been a concentrated effort to deny any significant contribution by other than African Americans to jazz. Without denying their major contribution to the establishment and development of the music, it is important for historical accuracy to acknowledge the role of others in its development. Teachout cites the more accurate position held by Duke Ellington, a man familiar with racism.

As for Duke Ellington, the man who composed Black, Brown, and Beige he also told an interviewer in 1945:

> Twenty years ago, when jazz was finding an audience, it may have had more of a Negro character. The Negro element is still important. However, jazz has become a part of America. There are as many white musicians playing it as Negro…We are all working along more or less the same lines. We learn from each other. Jazz is American now. American is the big word.

Five decades later, cultural politicians for whom the word "American" has validity only when it lies on the far side of a hyphen are undermining this spirit. That jazz, the ultimate cultural melting pot, and arguably America's most important contribution to the fine arts, should have fallen victim to such divisive thinking is an especially telling index of the unhappy state of our culture at the end of the twentieth century (Teachout 1995:53).

It is unfortunate that those who indulge in "ethnic cheerleading" do not understand that ethnicity is a double-edged sword, one that divides as well as unites. The glory of America has been its eventual and persistent ability to unite and to live up to its motto, "Out of Many, One". The true history of culture of jazz reaffirms that unity. Those who argue otherwise do the music and the country a disservice.

Chapter Four

Africa as a Metaphor of Authenticity in Jazz

"When Chano Pozo came from Cuba that brought it all together".
—Dizzy Gillespie

In 1903, W.E.B. Dubois articulated a theme that inheres in the very essence of African American culture, namely, "the dual heritage of the black man in America". That heritage, African and European, is at root one of dual identity and a cause of a recurring crisis of identity, as DuBois went on to note. In a very real sense, the history of jazz has provided a dynamic model of the ever-changing tenor of that heritage as well as a running commentary on it. It has done so through the use of tropes of identity.

Tropes encapsulate a culture's essence. Whatever a culture may be, however it views itself, it expresses that self-perception in select images packed with powerful meanings. Jazz is no exception. It, too, has its own cultural modes of expression, its personal symbols and metaphors that encapsulate and convey identity. Moreover, the best of these tropes arc flexible and allow for the expression of changing concepts of self-identity.

"Africa" has been precisely that type of vehicle within jazz. It has served as a touchstone for gauging the state of the art as well as the self-image of its performers. Throughout jazz history, the concept of "Africa" has served as an index of authenticity. The less "African" and more "European" a performance, for example, the less likely jazz musicians are to find it acceptable. Conversely, the more authentic, even flawed, a performance, the more it is perceived to be approaching an African essence or "soul". Jazz musicians have been careful and correct in indicating that their music is not a result of inability or corruption in performance, but, rather, of choice. Two musical cultures consisting of related, but differing codes, have been captured in the contrastive metaphors "African" and "European". These terms have not, of course, remained static over time.

Tracing the manner in which these contrastive terms have changed in meaning in the course of jazz's history provides an intriguing insight into both the genesis and change of jazz style and its cultural relationship to the increasing consciousness of its performers. Insight into that dialectical relationship, moreover, promises to lead to increasing understanding of the manner in which artists reinterpret cultural vehicles in order to convey their own personal visions of reality to fellow community members.

Three periods of jazz history serve as examples of the power of the "Africa/European" contrast as well as its derived tropes: the early years, the bop "revolution", and the period of Black Nationalism. Each period has had a major impact on the music. Each resulted from change in the meaning of being black in America. Moreover, each conveyed that meaning through the music while, in turn, receiving clarification and validation of black identity through that same music. Significantly, and interestingly, the first two movements left clear and relatively unproblematic impressions on the music and its culture. The third began as perhaps the clearest and most ambiguous musical movement in terms of its overall musical and cultural significance. Perhaps it is so difficult to assess simply because it is so radically different in its fundamental premises. It tries to abolish the binary opposition between "Africa/Europe" that is essential to the production of jazz itself and to the souls of those "black folks" who created this Creole music (Szwed, in press).

For example, improvisation alone does not distinguish jazz from so-called "classical" music. Although improvisation is essential to jazz, only a relative handful of its practitioners have been improvisational geniuses: though many others have been competent in its execution, some have been uninspired imitators. What does distinguish jazz from all other music, even to the point of often being overlooked, are its African elements. Collier (1978:5) discusses some of these traits:

> In jazz, timbre is highly personal, and varies not only from player to player but from moment to moment in a given passage for expressive purposes, just as European players swell or diminish a note to add feeling. In jazz, pitch is flexible to a considerable degree, and in fact in some types of jazz certain notes are invariable and deliberately played "out of tune" by European standards. European music, at least in its standard form, is built on the distinction between major and minor modes. The blues, a major building block in jazz, is neither major nor minor; it exists in a different mode altogether. In jazz, the ground beat is deliberately avoided in the melody and must be established by some sort of separate rhythm section.

In addition to the African elements of pitch, timbre, and cross-rhythms, there is the social element of jazz. Jazz is a music that thrives on contact between performer and audience. No matter how much an artist protests, few if any jazz performers actually sound better in studio recordings as opposed to "live" jazz performances. Indeed, most jazz musicians will entreat the audience to come closer in order to have them participate in a mutual act of creativity.[8]

These African elements have become so much a part of jazz that aside from discussions of "blue note" and rhythm, they tend to be overlooked. There has been no major innovation in jazz that has not been inspired and accompanied by rhythmic changes, inevitably in an African direction. Included in that category is the jazz triplet, which Jellyroll Morton used to term "the Spanish tinge".[9]

The Early Years

In common with most western music, jazz structurally comprises melody, harmony, and rhythm. Somewhat simplistically, it has been common to assign its harmony to Europe, its rhythm to Africa, and to leave its melody somewhat up for grabs. Although there is some truth in this stereotype, it excludes rather more than it includes. It is much more productive to leave the matter open to investigation even if the reality, or our ability to approximate it, proves less amenable to easy categorization than the myth it replaces (see Mensah 1983; Blacking 1983; Ladzekpo and Ladzekpo 1983).

And jazz, in common with every other culture, has its own myths, both internal and external; that is, myths its members generate to encapsulate and explain reality as well as myths outsiders have imposed upon it. Although both myths serve purposes, each type requires hermeneutical

---

[8] Art Blakey's comment is representative of the prevailing view in jazz: "I admit the band was sloppy at times, but I'd like to have heard somebody out swing us. Anyway, you oughtn't get too perfect in jazz it gets artificial. You've got no room."

[9] Marsalis (1986) and Gillespie (1979) are only two of many practicing jazz musicians who have insisted on the priority of rhythm in effecting meaningful stylistic changes in jazz. There are many technical reasons for rhythm's central role in jazz style. However, in this paper I am focusing on its symbolic significance. Simply put, as jazz moves toward more harmonic complexity it must reassert its rhythmic ties to Africa.

explication in order to yield deeper, rather than mere surface meanings.[10] Jazz, itself grew up out of the myth of Africa prevailing at the turn of the century. Many authors have waxed eloquent on the ways in which "Africa" has been used to provide the western world with its images. Hammond and Jablow (1977), for example, provide a useful introduction to the topic. Coetzee (1987:19) remarks:

> For centuries, in fact, it has been the fate of Africa to be employed by the west as a kind of image bank from which emblems—sometimes of savagery, brutality, and hopelessness, sometimes of innocence, simplicity and good nature—sometimes ... can be drawn at will. Mudimbe presents the best and most sophisticated treatment of this theme, the Western invention of Africa. His calm philosophical treatment exposes the process through which "Africa" came to be invented and the consequences for Africa and the west of its invention.

Whatever the "prehistory" of jazz may have been, jazz itself begins with the consequences of the imposition of Jim Crow laws in New Orleans and the subsequent cultural clash between black Creoles and other blacks in New Orleans. Until the application of these laws, late in the nineteenth century, white and black musicians routinely performed together.

The European/African tension, therefore, so vital to jazz itself, is not something simply imposed from outside. Neither is it something that exists between jazz and an outside culture, nor is it ever settled once and for all. The meaning of the key terms, "African" and "European", keep changing and are constantly renegotiated—even in each performance. Rather, it is a theme within its very core, a contradiction, or opposition, present in its own inception, a phenomenon not rare in colonial and post-colonial Africa itself (Mudimbe 1988). Within that dichotomy, "Africa" has come to represent total freedom, however freedom has come to be defined within America at any given time. Jazz's origin myth neatly emphasizes that connection. Presumably, Buddy Bolden one day simply picked up his cornet and began playing whatever he felt like, louder and higher than anyone else. Promptly, he became crowned as "King" Buddy Bolden. Eventually, he went insane from the fast-paced life his adulation thrust upon him. Unfortunately, no records exist of King Buddy, only embroidered memories. Certainly, his life has become a model for popular

---

[10] Sidron argues cogently that the cultural history of jazz is the history of black/white relations in this country. Furthermore, he calls for further studies exploring this theme. This work is, therefore, a belated response to his call, in the true spirit of jazz.

understanding of the jazz hero. The fact that there may have been no Buddy Bolden, or that there were a number of cornetists called Buddy Bolden will do nothing to dispel belief in the literal truth of the story. The symbolic truth, however, is even more important.

Creoles had sought to separate themselves from their fellow blacks, identifying themselves as black Europeans. Those Creoles who were musically inclined tended to perform European music in whatever "dignified" settings they could, including concert halls. Their subsequent bitterness and alienation is therefore best understood in terms of their sense of betrayal when New Orleans, a city they had felt to be somehow above race consciousness and open to advancement through cultural evolution, joined the rest of the South in imposing segregation based on race, rather than culture.

"Bolden", whoever he may have been, came to represent something different in music, something transitional between black folk music and European refrains. No matter how different, however, he never lost his identity, that identity that had its roots in Africa. I find it significant that in the legend he goes insane, for the strain of maintaining this marginal, ambiguous identity proves to be too much. It also places his music squarely in the Levi-Straussian category of the sacred.

From its inception, then, "Africa" has represented freedom within the jazz community. That freedom, of course, has been variously interpreted throughout the course of jazz's history precisely in terms Sidron (1981) has outlined; namely, within the context of black/white relationships. In the early days, that freedom was represented in the legendary figure of the free-living, loud, Buddy Bolden, driven insane by the failure of the world to recognize his genius. That genius was a "primitive" one, inherent, unteachable. And so the myth grew up of jazz being played without any rules, except those of a performer's own making, based on his own feelings. Presumably, it was an innate part of the jungle rhythms lurking, or resting, within every black. Needless to say, black musicians themselves often promulgated the myth, sometimes in an unsuccessful effort to keep whites from initiating their music.[11]

---

[11] Collier provides a clear exposition of this topic. It is interesting to note how little attention jazz critics and scholars have paid to the influence of black Creoles in shaping jazz. Certainly, anyone who heard Louis Armstrong in performance should have been aware of their influence, for he mentioned it frequently. Jelly Roll Morton, Barney Bigard, and Sidney Bechet spoke frequently of their "French" roots and Duke Ellington reportedly employed Bechet and Bigard to get that New Orleans Creole feeling in the music. Bechet eventually moved to France to get

The reality, predictably, was much different. Jones (1967), Taylor (1982), Collier (1978), Gridley (1978), Szwed (in press), and many others have tried to clarify the processes that led in the United States to jazz and in other areas to analogous Creole music. In the United States, as Jones (1967) has most eloquently argued, black Creoles in New Orleans represented a well trained, European cadre of musicians, culturally identifying themselves with white Europeans. These men had a clear understanding of the "proper" methods of performing European music and tended to be trained in that performance. As Taylor (1982) and Collier (1978) have argued, black musicians have always had an internal battle over the appropriate balance between African and European elements in the music. Those elements did not come from outside the community but from Black advocates of one strain or the other. The true geniuses of the genre were those rare stylists who combined both stylistic elements in their styles in unique combinations.[12]

Whites, even those who loved and admired jazz, often missed this point and, consequently, misunderstood its very structured nature. New Orleans jazz, for example, featured group improvisation. Such improvisation, however, was possible only because certain rather rigid rules operated. Among these rules was the fact that each of the melody instruments (cornet, or trumpet, clarinet, and trombone) stayed out of one another's way. The cornet or trumpet played the melody. The trombone provided bass harmony, and the clarinet supplied ornamentation, weaving its way between the brass instruments. Much like the "ideal" African village, it was an example of freedom within regulated limits, not surprisingly like a Bach Two- or Three-Part Invention.

Unrestrained freedom, in imitation of white perceptions of black African freedom, came to be found in the Chicago school of jazz. There, white musicians misunderstood what New Orleans musicians were really doing. For them, group improvisation meant that every melody instrument played the melody. Certainly, their misunderstanding proved a "happy accident", for it is problematic whether it really was part of the mainstream or merely an interesting example of "specific evolution". It

---

closer to his roots. The French concept of the évoluée obviously preceded and transcended its African empire.

[12] Collier 1978 (69) provides a brief discussion of the Bolden legend. He cites Samuel B. Charters as stating that there were many musicians named Buddy Bolden in early New Orleans jazz. One was still playing in 1908, a year after Buddy Bolden's presumed tragic death. Marquis, however, maintains that there was, in fact, an historical Buddy Bolden and offers impressive documentation to support his case.

would be interesting to explore related cultural developments, such as the art world's "discovery" and misunderstanding of African art. These misunderstandings proved equally fortuitous for western art, as Picasso and Braque amply demonstrated. The 1920s' infatuation with "Harlem" and other black centers was often an infatuation with its image of those centers rather than their realities, or at least the reality experienced by their residents.

Swing

Certainly, Armstrong's revolution in jazz rhythm falls into that tradition. So revolutionary was Armstrong's playing that the jazz trumpet innovator Miles Davis has stated that there is nothing done today on the trumpet that does not owe a debt of gratitude to something Armstrong did first. Certainly, Armstrong was the first great soloist in jazz and turned jazz into a predominantly soloist's art (Collier 1983:160). Of course, his great sense of melodic form played a major role in his success, for arguably no jazz musician since has ever constructed more perfectly structured melodic solos. But it is doubtful whether that sense of melody alone would have proved sufficient to have ushered in a new era of jazz.

What Armstrong did was to increase the feel for cross-rhythms in jazz while literally rewriting melodic lines. It is simply wrong to assert that he merely played the melodies as written, inserting perhaps a few ornamentations here and there. Moreover, his improvisations were not simply melodic, they ran the full gamut of African characteristics: pitch, timbre, falsetto leaps, melismatic vocalizations, terminal vibratos, and, above all, adaptations of African cross-rhythms.

Without neglecting the personal factor, the consideration of Armstrong as one of jazz's true improvisational geniuses, it is essential to investigate the relationship between his art and the times. Why, in other words, did jazz change from a group art to essentially a solo art form when it did? When jazz began, somewhere around the turn of the century, it did so in reaction to the imposition of Jim Crow laws in New Orleans, a town that had been relatively open racially and had allowed unprecedented intercourse, social and otherwise, between the races. Jim Crow not only tended to segregate black and white, it also forced conservative Creoles into contact with the poor "street" blacks whom they looked down upon (Jones 1967). The group improvisations of early New Orleans jazz can be viewed, in a very significant sense, as a means for stating the need for racial unity among blacks at a time of great sociocultural threat. Without stretching the point too much, it was music of solidarity in which each performer supported the others while staying out of their way.

But much had changed in America between the turn of the century and the early twenties. Although it was still a segregated society, World War I had allowed at least a glimpse of new opportunities. Too much has been made of the close of Storyville in New Orleans as the cause of the spread of jazz "up the Mississippi". The close of the notorious red light district by the U.S. Navy was more symbolic than substantial in signifying the movement of jazz from the Crescent City. More significant, in fact, in the migration of jazz was the movement of many blacks to the north as a result of economic opportunities consequent on U.S. entry into World War I.

Armstrong's migration certainly fits that model. He was sent for by his mentor, Papa Joe "King" Oliver and, for a time, continued to serve his apprenticeship with Oliver until it became apparent that his talent could not be contained as a second trumpet, even to Oliver. His abandonment of the cornet for the trumpet is an eloquent symbol of the changes in the music. Just as the earlier New Orleans style was primarily an ensemble one, Armstrong's music was primarily a soloist's music. It signaled at least the possibility of the emergence of individual blacks from the group and is consonant with the writing of DuBois, Langston Hughes, and the Harlem Renaissance, the stirring of independence in Africa, Marcus Garvey's Black Star Line and other post-war assertions of Black Pride.

It is merely wrong to treat Armstrong as a simple man who had no understanding of racial problems in the U.S. and whose music merely reiterated the myth of the "Happy Negro". Armstrong, in fact, had deep feelings regarding segregation and did take action on a number of occasions but, in general, his actions tended to be less dramatic than those of younger musicians. He had been born in a different time and tended like Duke Ellington to let his music talk for him. Certainly, at least in the twenties, it did just that (see Salamone 1989 for a discussion of the subversive nature of Armstrong's humor and the manner in which he used it to present an African-American perspective on American reality).

It was clear that he was his own man. His solos were commentaries that expressed the meaning of pop material to an African American. Armstrong reworked the material, making his own variations on the theme, thereby in his way making works of beauty from often banal melodies as Mozart did, for example with, "Twinkle, Twinkle Little Star". Indeed, Armstrong's music illustrates the entire approach-withdrawal dialectic of jazz. His use of "pop" material only served to emphasize the ambivalent position of Blacks within American culture, for when Armstrong played anything—even later in life when he was presumably past his creative peak— that piece was no longer ever heard in quite the same way again. He managed to force people to look at the familiar in a new way, the way that he as a black person looked at it. Perhaps, even more importantly the emergence of the jazz soloist made it possible for others to sing their songs and, thereby, present their views more forcefully.

Without denigrating the contributions of other early pioneers like Jelly Roll Morton or Sidney Bechet, without Armstrong it is difficult to imagine the emergence of the Swing Band. Before his innovations, technically the freeing of the solo from the ground beat and moving towards a more African approach to rhythm, big bands tended to clunk along, at best applying European understanding of syncopation to jazz. Since jazz's swing is not the result of syncopation, the result was usually rather pathetic, when not merely outright hilarious. It is often stated that Armstrong learned a great deal from his stint with Fletcher Henderson's band. He certainly did, but it is equally certain that Henderson applied what he learned from Armstrong to get the big band to swing and virtually all other big band arrangers applied his lessons to their work.

Throughout the big band period the lessons of Armstrong and Henderson were applied, modified and extended by others, like Duke Ellington, Count Basie, and Art Tatum. However, these lessons soon entered the public domain and were assimilated by white musicians as earlier innovations had been. Inevitably, it was these white musicians who reaped the popular rewards while the African American creators often fell victim to Jim Crow laws.

That tension caused the music to change. Black musicians were outspokenly aware that their music had been stolen from them. Benny Goodman became the "King of Swing" playing Fletcher Henderson's arrangements. No one really blamed Goodman: he knew the music's history and gave credit to his sources. Goodman did as much as anyone could to integrate the music in the 1930s. But that could not really compensate an artist for being neglected. Imitation may be the sincerest form of flattery but it is a poor substitute for fame and fortune.

Thus, black musicians worked at perfecting styles that were uniquely their own. No other band could imitate the swing of the Basie band. No other band could be mistaken for Ellington's. His sophisticated use of harmonies and tone colors, inspired by French impressionistic music and painting was unique in jazz. Black soloists rarely had equals among white musicians.

Those musicians who were indeed originals, like Bunny Berrigan or Bix Beiderbecke, found themselves imitating their own African myth, one stressing outrageous living, unreliability and self-centeredness as prerequisites for creativity. It was but one more version of the myth of the "Noble Savage", documented by Hammond and Jablow (1977), and enshrined in turn-of-the century novels like *She*, by H. Rider Haggard, and *Prester John*, by John Buchan. Eventually, then, out of the anger and pride of black musicians, out of a need to be credited with their own self-expression came a new type of jazz, Bop. Bop was a logical development of swing, but one that reflected the experience of blacks raised in the Depression who matured during World War II. These young men had seen the creative power of their music, seen others receive acclaim for it, and knew their own value—a value World War II was making eminently clear. Bop did not grow up to exclude whites (Bob Redcross, personal communication). Rather, it excluded the incompetent. It was music of fun in which the element of playing was stressed.

To those like Dizzy Gillespie, that playfulness took on rhythmic forms. It is just merely wrong to concentrate on the harmonic aspects of Bop and state that before Parker, Gillespie and the other Bop pioneers there were no harmonic improvisations in jazz. A simple listening to Coleman Hawkins's "Body and Soul", or any Art Tatum performance would upset such a contention. However, without ignoring the different harmonic conceptions of modern performers, for those who were involved in the creation of the new music it was the rhythm that was different (Gitler 1985:5).

Bop and Beyond: the Myth of Africa

When I asked Dizzy Gillespie how important Africa was for jazz, he removed the trumpet mouthpiece from his lips: "Very important. When Chano Pozo came from Cuba, it all came together."

Chano Pozo was an Afro-Cuban drummer raised in the Yoruba tradition, who came to play with Dizzy Gillespie in the United States in 1947. His work was of great interest to musicians, for along with other Afro-Cuban and African drummers he provided a symbol of Africa. His "romantic" death at the hands of someone who shot him in a dispute over narcotics money further seems to have enhanced his image. The fact that he was a Santeria who had run off with initiation money and died a year to the day later added an additional African tinge to the story (see Gillespie 1979:347-48).

Throughout the post-war era, Africa's aura grew among jazz musicians. Certainly, the independence movement added to Africa's mystique and the linkage of Black Liberation with it was only natural. Islam became common among musicians long before it spread to other segments of the

African American community. Armstrong's trip to Ghana was merely the most noticeable of many trips by jazz musicians to the continent. Africa increasingly became a metaphor of authenticity, of true identity within the black musical community.

The central question to be addressed in this final section is why the one movement that openly embraced Africa as a symbol of Black Power is the one that has been least popular both within the musical community and with its fans.

Certainly, images of Africa have long been part of jazz history. As I have argued, the contrast between "Africa" and "Europe" has provided dialectic of development for jazz itself. African elements have always formed part of the musical composition of jazz, and "jungle" images, for better or worse, have been used, willingly or not, by Ellington and others. Many musicians have become Muslims in a belief that Islam is a more authentic African religion than Christianity and, thus, more appropriate for an African American.

In the 1960s, however, Black Nationalism became more openly dominant in jazz than it had ever been before, in conformity with the self-conscious assertion of the right of blacks to control their own destiny, including their own identity. As America in general entered the confrontational politics of the late sixties, themes of identity—youth, gays, women, and blacks—became more pronounced. Initially, these assertions of identity tended to be separatist and exclusionary. The movement illustrated a very interesting contrast between black and white images of Africa in jazz. White musicians *choose* to be part of black culture; they are, however, free to move in and out of it at will. They are, therefore, always on trial by black musicians and are aware of their probationary status. They tend to be both more romantic and fanatic about the mystique of Africa than black musicians who are more likely to use the concept as a tool—even as a weapon—in order to obtain their objectives.

There were a number of manifestations of the movement to Africanize jazz. In some way, jazz was to be made "free". Indeed, even before the Black Power movement itself had jelled, Ornette Coleman had come on the scene in 1959 and, after an initial burst of enthusiasm, met with outright hostility. Within a few short years, however, many of his basic ideas were being followed.

But the harmony was another matter. Here, freedom was king. The chord changes were ignored, and the player was really free to introduce what often appeared to be foreign elements, some of them simple cries and grunts. Coleman's playing in general tends to stay within a very limited harmonic compass (Collier 1978:467). Freedom became associated with what many musicians considered a step back in music history, a return to simpler harmony, presumably closer to African roots. The soloist became freer to concentrate on melodic statements, or thematic development. Coleman often speaks somewhat mystically of development of emotions or feelings. It is interesting to note that his metrical work, in contrast with his theme of freedom, is very rigid. Almost all his work is in the thirty-two bar popular song structure.

However, even those who are harmonically very astute moved in the 1960s to a simpler harmonic base. In this respect, the movement to modes can be interpreted as a movement to be "free". Up until this period, the dominant movement in music was toward increasing complexity, exemplified in the triumph of bop and early post-bop. There was the dominance of the blazingly fast John Coltrane on saxophone, who played every possible note in every possible chord change in his later 1950s "sheets of sound" period. Although he could play creatively in this style until his untimely death in 1966, he virtually abandoned post-bop and became increasingly involved in the free jazz movement.

That movement was interested in giving the individual as complete a freedom as possible in order to allow nothing to get between his message and the audience. That quest for freedom, part of the broader political and artistic movement of the sixties, led to a return to modal and other types of playing that stressed melodic and thematic development without binding the performers to strict adherence to set or altered chord progressions. Just as "black" was being proclaimed beautiful in defiance of the dominant æsthetics of the past, so, too, were new sounds being explored for their potential beauty, even if, or, perhaps, especially if "experts" had termed them ugly. Towards that end the turn to modes is quite logical.

Modes are scales presumably modeled on Greek music used in the Middle Ages for choral music. They were generally abandoned as the New Music came to dominate European practice, and as harmony became more and better understood in practice and theory. The fact that modal music was associated with vocal music is, I think, a major factor in its emergence during a period of time when Black Nationalism was being vocal. I believe the pun was intentional. The soloist was to be freer to sing a song (vocalize) and to deliver a message (to be vocal).[13]

The move was also seen by many to be a return to one's roots; that is, Africa. There were many other currents in the jazz styles of the period that reflected this concern. In retrospect it is clear that they all were related in

---

[13] Kofsky 1983, original 1970, is still the best work on the meaning of the music to the Black Power movement as well as to the internal workings of the music itself. It is a powerful and clear Marxist statement of the role of art in a revolution.

an attempt to "get back to Africa", the source of authentic identity. The path taken in "Free" jazz eventually was through harmonic simplification coupled with rhythmic sophistication. The purpose was 'to tie changes in the music to changes in society'. In other words superfluous westernizations were to be stripped out of the music in order to leave it more "purely African".

Leaving aside the irony of returning to pseudo-Greek modes created to write church music, such as Gregorian chant, it is also problematic whether African-music is, in fact, as limited harmonically as many musicians have tended to assume. The purpose, however, of "free" jazz was to change one's perspective on the music through freeing the soloist from slavery to harmonic chord changes and forcing him to view new possibilities in the music. The soloist was free to solo on a line as long as he wanted without having to change to new chords and thereby tell his story without "western" constraints. All sounds were created equal in this "free" music. There were no dominants, no tonics—only freedom.

It is in this sense only that one can talk about the emergence of an "eastern" influence in jazz at this period. That influence never rivaled an African one and was part of the Third World ideology put forward by Archie Shepp and others who were Black Nationalists within the profession. Shepp noted that all oppressed people were people of color and his brothers. Certainly, very few musicians were wearing Indian clothing at this time but many, even in the mainstream, wore dashikis. Coltrane's albums and individual compositions were replete with African references as were many others not so committed to freedom in the music, or who did not define it in the same way. Certainly, the new music did offer new perspectives and many of its accomplishments have entered mainstream jazz. It did, in fact, often imitate its conception of early New Orleans

One avant-garde musician stated that one of his goals was to attain that type of group improvisation common in early New Orleans music (Kaeef Ruzadun, personal communication). Of course, group improvisation was possible in that style because of its close adherence to harmonic theory. In contrast, the music was limited harmonically and featured repetition and explicit messages. Although its major figures included many who were harmonically sophisticated, such as John Coltrane, many of its adherents were not aware of the harmonic requirements of modes or of their restrictions. Indeed, it is useful to realize that many harmonically sophisticated jazz musicians were rather ambivalent about "free" jazz. Even John Coltrane and Eric Dolphy drifted in and out of the movement and recorded tonal music until their deaths. In fact, the only truly creative "free" musicians, with the possible exception of Ornette Colman, were those who were already harmonically adept, such as Don Cherry, Bill Evans, John Coltrane, Miles Davis, McCoy Tyner, Pharaoh Sander, and their ilk. Most of these musicians eventually returned to tonal music, for not only could white musicians play free, but many conservatory-trained black and white musicians were also rather old hat in conservatory music. Many also pointed out that freedom in jazz is found within the tension of its constraints. Drummer Elvin Jones has eloquently expressed this position in interviews with Frank Kofsky (1977 and 1978): "I wasn't thinking anything about style. It was just a reaction to what was going on. However, a style just seems to develop and I just reacted to whatever I heard; that's my style, I suppose" (1978:82).

From his interview with Jones, Kofsky reaches some rather insightful conclusions regarding revolutions in general and the revolution of "free" jazz in particular. Two of these insights are relevant to the major premise of this paper. Therefore, I shall quote at some length:

> ...revolutions do not annihilate tradition so much as they do recast and record its most valuable elements in ways that revitalize the tradition itself (1977:11). I would deduce that the only way to proceed further along the path that Jones had already begun exploring, one that led towards the recreation of African polyrhythms, would have necessitated the abandonment of certain fundamental conventions that heretofore had prevailed in jazz—in particular, the principles that all musicians acknowledge a common measure-line and that a single predetermined meter (or rarely-meters) be sustained unaltered throughout the performance, regardless of how much rhythmic displacement has been created within that meter—and might also have required the presence of additional percussionists, perhaps playing in different and even variable meters within the Coltrane ensemble (1977:29).

Such a movement would have led to the end of jazz (Kofsky 1977:30) and Jones resisted it, leaving Coltrane and even, more or less, "free" jazz, often playing much more conventional styles. It is important to note that the myth of African roots if taken too literally, as Coltrane is asserted in Kofsky's article to have done, can kill the culture itself, as it would have done to jazz. The tension of European and African elements is required for jazz to exist, for the trope of jazz is about just that: a culture that is neither "this" nor "that", but somehow "this *and* that". In Levi-Strauss's terms, it belongs to an anomalous category and is somehow sacred. This binary opposition between polar forces is essential to the survival of the form. As jazz performers move in one direction, it is necessary that there be a compensatory movement in another direction in order to maintain the tensional integrity of the music.

Indeed, there was a great irony in the pose of great seriousness on the part of many of the avant-garde's leading lights, for it seriously contrasted with the usual African attitude toward music, and was a throwback to the European heritage of black Creole music performance. Indeed, the hushed concert halls and rapt attention these performers demanded, at least in their rhetoric, smack more of the ideal European concert hall than of any African clearings I have visited. Radano (1976:77) clearly sums up the meaning of the jazz avant-garde and their relationship with the jazz community of musicians and fans:

> ...these angry critics and musicians claimed to carry the torch for the new black society. They declared themselves dedicated to restoring "blackness" to jazz, to toppling the power structure of clubs and record companies, and to bringing to the black population a music that they considered rightfully its own... what they failed to recognize—or refused to admit—was the elitist character of avant-garde jazz. By nature, avant-garde jazz is not music for the masses—black or white... Musical norms operate like all other social norms—they change slowly... The real culprit was jazz itself. While the avant-garde musicians identified with jazz and the jazz community, they themselves remained a separate community... the members of the jazz avant-garde were 'cultivated' musicians trapped in a 'vernacular' milieu.

Conclusions

Rhythm, harmony, and melody alone cannot explain tonal western music. Therefore, an *a fortiori* resort to any single aspect of this trinity in an attempt to explain jazz is too narrow to provide more than a glimpse of what jazz means. Even study of the interaction of these musical elements, a far more promising, but also less pursued, research avenue, is insufficient to reveal the rich semiotic implications of jazz. For jazz is not totally a tonal western music. Nor does it merely comprise rhythm, harmony, and melody. It has a rich stock of other elements, replenished throughout its history, that its practitioners label "African". Moreover, one simply misses the point through confusing a structure with the message that that structure conveys.

In one very real and important sense, jazz itself is the message. Its own meaning, to its practitioners and fans, changes over time as its social location alters and as the meaning of its "African/European" opposition varies. However, the situation is further complicated because each jazz musician and performance is meant to be creative, to generate meaning. Over and over, in one form or other, the principle is laid down that each musician must tell a story. Moreover, that story must be personal: one must live the story the music tells. In a truly essential way the medium is the message. Technique, for example, the ability to run chord changes accurately, to play fast or slow and still swing, is admired, but only a naïve listener admires it for its own sake. It must be used in the service of conveying a story. Charlie Parker, for example, is said to have advised aspiring saxophone players to first learn everything about their horns and then to forget it all when playing. Technique, in other words, is only a tool in allowing one's true inner self to be expressed: it is not admirable in and of itself. A knowledgeable insider sums up the position well when speaking about the early days of the bop revolution: "I never heard anyone play as fast as Bird. But it wasn't just speed. He had ideas no one else had" (Bob Redcross, personal communication).

Endeavoring to understanding the meaning of jazz, therefore, involves one in a series of exercises requiring the examination of multiple referents and cross-referents, of matching individual biographies to broader movements, specific variations to broader themes, and the ever-retreating just out of reach essence of the metaphor that is jazz itself, for to understand jazz is to understand the tertium quid that it is; namely, a symbol and encapsulation of America itself.

CHAPTER FIVE

THE CULTURE OF JAZZ AND JAZZ AS CRITICAL CULTURE

Who knows but that, on the lower frequencies, I speak for you?
—Ralph Ellison, Invisible Man

Neil Leonard states, "For all true believers jazz answered needs that traditional faith did not address. While the music had different meanings for different followers—black, white, male female, young, old, rich or poor, in various psychological states and social situations—for all devotees it provided some form of ecstasy or catharsis transcending the limitations, dreariness and desperation of ordinary existence".

Moreover, he continues:

As earthy blues, exalted anthem, or something in between, jazz could energize the most jaded will. Jazz is an active agent, a powerful force whose ecstasies, whether subtly insinuated or supplied in lightening illuminations, altered personality and society. Through cajolery, charm, warmth, surprise, shock or outrage it could brush aside the most entrenched tradition, the most oppressive custom, and inspire subversive social behavior. Consider how the jazzy music of the twenties went hand in hand with the upheavals in manners and morals of that time, how bop was the cry of street-wise young rebels in the forties, and how the "New Thing" of the sixties was closely allied to the "Black Power" impulse of the day. Clearly, jazz is more than a passive flower, a glorious cultural ornament affirming humanity, it is also a powerful social force which has cut broadly and deeply, its prophets, rituals and myths touching not only individual souls but large groups bringing intimations of magic and the sacred to an era whose enormous changes have depleted conventional faiths.

It is this power of jazz to propel social change and energize its acolytes, its touch of the sacred, which I wish to develop in this work.

Pratt (1990:7) notes that popular music in general has expressive and instrumental political functions. He quotes John Coltrane, a major jazz influence, as stating that a person's sound reveals his personality, the way he thinks and interprets the world (Sidran 1981:14). Pratt notes, correctly, that in performance that interpretation may change. Indeed, jazz performance is one in which fellow musicians and the audience sway the musician, providing at times new insights and facets on reality. This openness in jazz is one of its hallmarks, and jazz musicians often cite it as a sacred characteristic.

In conformity with the sacred nature of jazz role reversal and rituals of rebellion are common modes of behavior and communication. Armstrong's demonstration of the power of music and humor to subvert pompous platitudes regarding the established order of things provides an entrée to the theoretical relationship between music and humor and the uses to which an accomplished artist may put that relationship. This scared trickster quality was an integral part of Louis Armstrong's persona, one that he was well aware of and used with consummate skill to comment on and subvert mainstream conception of reality. An example of this power of subversion explodes from his recording of "Laughin' Louie".

Laughin' Louie

There are a number of jokes on "Laughin' Louie". The first joke is the fact that Armstrong always referred to himself as "Louis". He joked that white folks always pronounced his name as "Louie". In fact, on one poster his name is wrongly spelled "Lewis", obviously following his own pronunciation. So it is not a far stretch to see the title as Armstrong laughing at those who think they are superior but cannot even pronounce his name correctly.

What else is Louis laughing at? Well, he is laughing at the fact that he and his Vipers recorded "Laughin' Louie" while high on marijuana. In 1931 Armstrong was high much of the time and "viper" was a slang expression for a pothead (Bergreen 1997:332, 360). The fact that he could use the expression for his band, and even for his tune "Song of the Vipers", was but another in-joke on Satchmo's part at the expense of polite society.

Additionally, to many people's amazement, Armstrong liked the Guy Lombardo big band sound. In 1931, Armstrong was fronting a "sweet" big band, one that featured whining saxophones as well as strict adherence to playing the melody the way it was written. At the same time, the band was reminiscent of Paul Whiteman's in including "hot" players. The mixture of Armstrong's melodic but hot trumpet over the sweet sound of his trumpet is often funny. Whether Satchmo intended it to be humorous or not is arguable, but it has its unique charm and humor in any case. It does contrast an overly up-tight style of music with a looser and even more sophisticated one. It also contrasts a mistaken notion of a "correct" way to play jazz that fits all musicians with his own, catholic, tastes.

Of course, the joke could just as well be on the hipsters who put down Guy Lombardo's music. Armstrong, along with other jazz musicians, is an innate fusionist. They merge all sorts of music into jazz, adapting it to the idiom. Throughout his life, Armstrong flatly stated that he liked Lombardo's music. It is there in his music, just as Puccini's arias are there.

The New Orleans tradition is a Creole one that delights in mixing categories in a rich gumbo. It is also clear that in this period Armstrong was reveling in Black Culture and eager to share it with his audience. He included a great deal of inside jokes in his versions of popular songs. For example, his version of Hoagy Carmichael's "Old Rocking Chair" contains this response to Jack Teagarden's vocal statement that he is going to tan Louis's hide, "My hide's already tanned, Father!" Furthermore, Teagarden was white, a white trombonist who was slightly older than Armstrong and had early recognized his genius. The two had been close friends since the 1920s and cooperated in mocking racial stereotypes. The sly reference to miscegenation, a taboo subject in mixed company, slid by the censors.

Armstrong gave white audiences a peak at black entertainment by performing vaudeville routines featuring a stock character, the corrupt black preacher, and many versions have been recorded. He referred often to his love for New Orleans food, early poverty, and details of black life. He turned them all into gentle jokes so that he could get on with his own love for life and over his own pain. Moreover, Armstrong mocked received opinion about the dangers of pot smoking through his viper jokes. Many in his audience did not know that "viper" was a nickname for pot and its users. "Laughin' Louie" is filled with Armstrong's famous nonsense words, stammering, and bar after bar of laughter. Again, one asks what the joke is.

Armstrong is Br'er Rabbit, again laughing at those who seek to best him. Armstrong was able to survive during the Depression when the market for "race records", those records aimed primarily at a black audience, had ended. He did so by following in the footsteps of other black performers, using race humor to his advantage.

There is a long history of Africans and African Americans using humor to overcome hardships and to subvert ideas that endanger their survival. The use of humor, of course, offers a deniability of malice. The phrase "only kidding" was one that Armstrong often used. The article "African-American Humor" in Aileen. Pace Nilsen and Don L.F. Nilsen's

Encyclopedia of 20th Century American Humor (2000) offers numerous examples of this practice.

In west Africa, the original home of more than 50 per cent of American slaves, anthropologists have found cultures with many of the same characteristics that African Americans rely on for their humor: extensive wordplay and punning, signifying (verbal put downs), the mocking of an enemy's relatives, the chanting and singing of ridicule verses, bent-knee dancing, an admiration for the trickster, and aggressive joking that demands verbal quickness and wit (Nilsen and Nilsen 2000:14). Salamone (1990), Keil (1979, 1992), and Crouch (2000), among others, have also noted similarities in the use of humor among Africans and African-Americans, and more particularly they have noted this similarity among African Americans and African musicians.

Dizzy Gillespie—Crazy Like a Fox

Dizzy Gillespie, for example, continued the trickster tradition in jazz. Dizzy, born John Birks Gillespie in 1917 was given his nickname early in his career. The bandleader Teddy Hill gave him the nickname because of his crazy antics on stage. For example, Dizzy used to come to rehearsals dressed in a hat, gloves, and overcoat, which he kept on throughout the rehearsal no matter the temperature. However, Hill always added, "Diz crazy? Diz was crazy like a fox." He claimed, quite rightly, that Diz was a stable person, "the most stable of us all." Hill, as most jazz musicians, thought quite highly of Diz. He gave him his first recorded solo and featured him at Minton's Playhouse, one of the fabled "birthplaces" of be-bop.

It is important to note that Dizzy's humor was not common among his fellow modernists. In fact, as he later acknowledged, it was related to the type of humor that Louis Armstrong used because he was such a great showman. Many modern musicians, who acted "cool", turning their backs on their audiences and failing to acknowledge applause or announce tunes, put down Armstrong as an "Uncle Tom" whose antics kept jazz in the show business category. They want jazz to be considered high art in a league with classical music and separate from entertainment. Diz, who was a close friend of Armstrong's, used humor to draw people to the new jazz. Even though both Diz and Satch recorded parodies of the other's music, their uncanny ability to reproduce it showed they had listened closely to it. Indeed, material in the Louis Armstrong archives shows that his taste in music included not only opera, classics, pop tunes, but the most modern of jazz recordings. His recorded comments while listening with musician friends, shows his ability to critique the musicianship of performers. He rated Gillespie quite highly on all accounts.

Just as Armstrong used humor to bring his superb music to audiences that had not heard his music before, so, too, did Gillespie. Audiences found humor, correctly, in the twists and turns of bop tunes and extended lines. If humor is built on surprise, then bop was an appropriate vehicle for humor. Charlie Parker is often caught on recordings, laughing out loud, especially when he and Diz played together and finished each other's phrases, as friends finish one another's jokes. Diz's dress was another humorous sales technique for bop. His infamous bop glasses, string ties, and, above all, his beret gave bop a sartorial identity, which all except squares found humorous. There was a trickster humor about bop, which many missed, although many sensed its subversive nature, questioning the status quo and seeking to replace old, unjust verities with new equitable ones. Bop was the musical language of the post-war African American but its roots went deeper than that. Try as some of its adherents did to deny the fact, it partook of the humor of the African trickster, just as Satchmo did and Gillespie came to admit he did as well.

The Trickster and the Diz

The trickster myth is found in clearly recognizable form among both aboriginal tribes and modern societies. We encounter it among the ancient Greeks, the Chinese, the Japanese, and in the Semitic world as well. Many of the trickster's traits were perpetuated in the figure of the mediæval jester, and have survived right up to the present day in the Punch-and-Judy plays and in the clown. Although repeatedly combined with other myths and frequently drastically reorganized and reinterpreted, its basic plot seems always to have succeeded in reasserting itself (Radin 1955:ix).

We have a fundamental figure here, which is both general and specific. There appears a general need for the trickster, but a need clothed in specific features of a culture. The trickster can be creator and destroyer, one who gives and one who takes, one who tricks and is tricked. The trickster inspires awe and affection at the same time. Seemingly, the trickster is one who gives into primal impulses without thinking. But I would argue that he is sly as a fox, which does, at least at times, clearly see the results of his behavior but who can get away with much because of his humor.

I have argued that powerful, sacred African figures require humor so that the audience can approach them (Salamone 1995:3-7; Salamone 1976:208-210). The informality prevalent in American jazz allows the royalty to temper the awe inherent in their status in order to permit youngsters to approach them. I suggest that much the same practice can be found in Nigeria. For example, I worked with a traditional priest who was one of the more powerful "doctors" in Nigeria. However, in order to encourage clients rather than discourage them, he cloaked his power beneath a persona of humor. This humorous presentation drew people to him whom he might otherwise have frightened away (Salamone 1976). Similarly, giants such as Count Basie and Duke Ellington have used humor in their presentations. Basie's "Pop Goes the Weasel" insert in "April in Paris", and Ellington's humorous raps in his introductions and in his retelling of fairy tales frequently warmed up the crowds.

Dizzy Gillespie and Louis Armstrong shared an ability to draw people to themselves. Doing so enabled them to work their music for the good of the people while being open to further innovations. Although the Bori was an African trickster, I have not gone on a diversion here.

I am explicitly suggesting that Gillespie and Armstrong, among others, are in that same tradition. They clearly used humor to draw people to them. They would do almost anything to make the audience receptive to their message, for their music did indeed have a message. For Gillespie and Armstrong before him, that music was, in fact, "spiritual". I once asked Dizzy about why he said it was spiritual: "Makes the other fellow sound good," he replied with his usual arch wit.

Additionally, there is an African tradition which holds that the musician has a sacred duty to stand up to oppression and speak the truth to power. In that task, Gillespie followed a long tradition of African musicians. It is no accident, I think, that the Yoruba musician Fela Anakulapi-Kuti studied and worked with Gillespie early in his career. Even Fela's claim to be the Black President has traces of Gillespie's half-humorous Presidential candidacy. Fela combined various aspects of African-based music into his style. Interestingly, its foundation was the jazz of Gillespie and Charlie Parker, which he heard as a young man and which he used to create something different for Nigerian music, something he deemed would be revolutionary. He put on a mask of the Trickster to perform. Mocking those whom he deemed had betrayed Africa, the colonialists and their African collaborators.

The Humor of Subversion

Dizzy would often open his performances by saying he would like to introduce the band. Band members would then turn to one another and shake hands, giving their names to each other, smiling and nodding. The routine, which I saw repeated many times, never got stale. Diz would sometimes stand aside and raise his eyebrows bemusedly at the audience. Eventually, he would get to introduce the musicians in the band, for Diz was a fair man who gave each person his due.

I remember one night in the winter of 1957-58 when he arrived in the middle of a blizzard to perform in Rochester, NY. He was late, something unusual for him. The audience, however, waited for him, knowing that somehow he'd make it through the storm. In those days, Diz traveled by car along the Birdland Circuit and he was coming in from Detroit. As the band scrambled to take off their heavy, snow-laden coats and assemble their instruments, Diz began to play solo trumpet.

The audience laughed as they recognized a current hit, "Tequila", by the Champs. They stopped laughing when they realized Diz had bested them again because he was playing it straight. He took the novelty tune and re-imagined it as a lovely then torrid Latin tune. One by one the band members joined in as they assembled their instruments.

After ten minutes or so, Diz then began his spiel. He apologized for being late: "I was playing a benefit for the Ku Klux Klan at the White Citizens' Hall in Montgomery Alabama." As the crowd broke up, he launched into "Manteca" (Grease) with his then new opening chant, "I'll never go back to Georgia. No, I'll never go back to Georgia." Again, as the crowd—and it was a crowd, despite the snow—roared with laughter, he launched into a brilliant high-note solo, complete with all the pyrotechnics of which he was capable in his prime.

I reminded Diz of this performance thirty years later when he was performing at Elizabeth Seton College. He remembered it with a smile and repeated the opening of his solo for me vocally. It was then that he talked about humor and the spirituality of music, among many other topics. Diz took his role as a teacher/musician seriously, reminding me of Chaucer's scholar "Gladly would he learn and gladly teach".

There was another routine he had when doing "Swing Low, Sweet Cadillac", his version of "Swing Low, Sweet Chariot". The song is not only an American spiritual, but, according to the saxophonist Archie Shepp, also comes from an African religious song. Diz began his version with a Yoruba chant from Chano Pozo, a Cuban Santeria. The chant often drew befuddled laughs from the audience, and Diz played it up big. For him, humor and spirituality were not polar opposites but complementary principles. Humor was a means of leading people to the spiritual.

As he told me, "When Chano Pozo came, the music all came together." Again, once Diz finished his chanting, also setting the cross-rhythms of his tempo, he started the song, in the midst of which he took a brilliant solo.

When the tenor sax player James Moody was present, there would be two brilliant solos. Then the piece would end with Dizzy's tag line, "Old Cadillacs never die. The finance company just tows them away!"

The examples could continue. Just what was this once wild bad boy of jazz getting at? What did his great dancing in front of his band mean? His mugging with his frog-like cheeks? His tilted bell on his horn? His African robes later in life? His pointedly supercilious vocabulary? His outrageous twists and turns, with his deeply serious playing on frivolous tunes and his humor on serious ones. What was he telling the audience? And just which audience was he addressing?

The following vignette displays most of the characteristics I have discussed.

One night in Texas in the mid-1950s (Kliment 1988:75-76), the incomparable Ella Fitzgerald was sitting backstage eating a sandwich and watching the band members playing dice, a group that included renowned trumpeter Dizzy Gillespie. Fitzgerald was terrified by the sudden arrival of local law officials, who arrested the entire group for gambling. The officers, upset because the group was performing in an all-white theater, took them to the police station where they were booked and jailed—Fitzgerald still in her ball gown. During the booking process, an officer asked Gillespie for his name. He replied, "Louis Armstrong."

And that is what the officer wrote down. Several hours later, after the band's white manager paid the $50 bail, an arresting officer asked Ella Fitzgerald for her autograph. The next day, local papers reported that she was the best-dressed prisoner the jail ever held (Iris Carter Ford:43).

The subversive quality which and Diz exemplified, the indistinguishability of the sacred and profane, the refusal to take accepted interpretations of reality at face value, the substitution of new realities for old are often found in literature based on jazz culture.

Jazz in Literature

In African American Satire: The Sacredly Profane Novel, Darryl Dickson-Carr writes of Wallace Thurman's Infants of the Spring:

> Infants of the Spring, then, asks us to reconcile what is normally considered an oxymoron, at least in the United States: an individualistic group consciousness... What... Thurman... demands, however, is actually a precursor to the conundra that Ralph Ellison would propose in his widely acclaimed Invisible Man Raymond argues that principles upheld by masses of African Americans are the ultimate linchpins to African Americans' cultural and political progress, not unlike the narrator of Invisible Man,

who argues that African Americans "were to affirm the principle on which the country was built", despite the reality of staunch, violent opposition, lest the nation, and therefore African Americans, be lost forever. It is precisely this fear of total loss, of an African American community swallowed up because it wastes its energies on frivolities instead of a fight for principles that drives Infants of the Spring's satire (Dickson-Carr 2001:56-57).

This satirical glance is common to jazz and literature based on jazz. Jazz is music of freedom and, as such, opposed to that which hinders freedom. Thus, it is the supporter of all that promotes freedom, although just what constitutes that freedom is open to debate. Indeed, sometimes it appears that everything is open to debate in the jazz world.

Although the origins of jazz as an essentially African American music are not seriously in doubt, the exclusivity of it as something only African Americans can perform *is* in doubt. I have written about it earlier (Salamone 1990). Indeed, I find the fact that some "white" players can sound as black as "black" players a significant cultural phenomenon and will return to it in the conclusion. Jürgen E. Grandt has similar thoughts.

In 1951, James Baldwin wrote that "... it is only in his music ... that the Negro of America has been able to tell his story" (24). But that same year, British jazz critic Leonard Feather published in the pages of Down Beat magazine a blindfold test with jazz trumpeter Roy Eldridge. Throughout his distinguished career, Eldridge had repeatedly expressed his firm belief that white and black jazz musicians had distinctly different styles and that he could easily distinguish between them. When Feather took him at his word and administered the test, the results were somewhat astonishing: The musician, nicknamed "Little Jazz" by his peers, was either noncommittal or wrong much more often than he was right (Feather, Book 47). Listening to Billy Taylor's recording of, ironically, "All Ears", the seventh of ten selections, Eldridge's irritation mounted. "I liked the pianist. Couldn't tell who was colored and who was white. They could be Eskimos for all I know," he admitted, and had to concede defeat in the end (Feather, "Little Jazz" 12). (1) Eldridge's blindfold test again raises the old yet still provocative question: Can white folks play the blues? If indeed the end product of a jazz performance transcends what W.E.B. Du Bois called "the problem of the color-line" (v)—can jazz itself still provide a useful critical framework for the study of black American cultural expressions? To be sure, music, instrumental music at least, is a much more abstract art form than literature, but the contemporary critic still faces the same dilemma that confronted Roy Eldridge: the apparent paradox that jazz music is at once a distinctly black American art form as well as a cultural hybrid. Jazz, indeed, in literature has taken on this hybrid, multicultural aspect. It is both "a distinctly black American art form as well as a cultural hybrid".

The point is that jazz is a Creole art form, which combines elements of seeming opposites, making reality a matter of "this" and "that too". Like American society and culture which it mirrors and shapes, jazz derives its power from its combination of opposites, which it combines into some new thing. That new thing appears to change constantly before our eyes, making any absolute understanding of reality but a tentative guess. Everything can be other than it is.

Such a perspective is a metaphor of American culture itself. It, too, is always in the process of becoming, rarely taking time to "be". Even the most banal themes can be transformed into things of exquisite beauty and at the most unexpected times. In the midst of despair, hope explodes into consciousness. America and jazz have grown up together and each expresses the fact that our seeming differences must be reconciled in a creative tension of harmony that can produce something far more beautiful and productive than their individual elements or else fall into broken fragments far inferior to those from which they came.

In literature, jazz has represented freedom. For those detractors of the music, it represented license and a return to the primitive with all that such a designation implied: namely, sexual license, indeed license of all types. For its literary supporters, Fitzgerald, Carl Van Vechten, and John Dos Passos, Claude McKay, Countee Cullen, Zora Neale Hurston, Langston Hughes, Richard Wright, and Jean Toomer as well as James, Baldwin, Jack Kerouac and Toni Morrison, the music is a force against fascism and other systems opposing freedom. It is a movement for racial integration and social justice. To emphasize their jazz roots, these writers used jazz accents and rhythms in their writings.

Multiple and Overlapping Realities and Audiences

The Eshu trickster from the Yoruba of Nigeria is a character who disturbs the peace by questioning norms and calling his people to be attentive skeptics of order. He also employs a crafty and cunning wit in the face of the more powerful, preserving his and others' freedom where it might potentially be curtailed. The Yoruba also parallel their trickster to the artist, celebrating his imaginative capacities and malleable skills. In all of these respects, Louis Armstrong may be regarded as a quintessential trickster, part of a long legacy passed from Africa and through slave-holding and segregated America.

In a broader context, Armstrong's trickster role can be tied to the jazz musical genre that he so transformed. Both were subject to—and responded to—unavoidable social realities, expressing pain and anger in reaction to a debilitating racism. Both also employed secret musical codes, employing protective masks that gave space to individual freedom and collective empowerment. Furthermore, both recognized humor as the license that permitted their liberationist expressions of thinly veiled social commentary. Jazz, like Armstrong, offered a language, the subtleties of which spoke to the in-crowd (the "hip") and about the outsiders (the "squares"). Invariably, it would privately mock either or both.

Louis Armstrong used the trickster image in his rendition of "Laughin' Louie". First, the "squares" are outed in the title itself, which parodies the common misinterpretation of his name in mainstream culture and mocks the one-dimensional stereotype with which he was regarded (and sometimes dismissed). From Armstrong's point-of-view, the title's humor might also allude to his habitual pot-smoking habits, this further underscored by the name of his accompanying band, the Vipers, a slang term for marijuana. The song's music fluctuates throughout, between the "hot" sound "hip" critics encouraged from Armstrong, and the "sweet" sounds he always had such affection for, but for which he was criticized as compromising to mainstream tastes. Here, the trickster celebrates his own creative choices (laughing for himself), and satirically dismisses the imposing judgment of his critics (laughing at them). This is achieved through the humorous method of incongruity, the shock of the juxtaposed styles surprising listeners into recognition and appreciation while appealing to many different audiences.

In considering audiences we must take note of the fact that Gillespie, as Armstrong before him, addressed multiple audiences. Indeed he was also a member of multiple audiences. As an African American southern musician he was always aware of his membership in Afro-American culture, his acculturation into the dominant white culture, his being a leading founder of bop, his maleness and many other memberships. His intelligence shone through as he played with these identities in his performances, juggling one against the other as the mood took him. Things were rarely, if ever, this *or* that; as Robert Farris Thompson (1964) has noted about Creole culture; they were this *and* that, too (see also Roger D. Abrahams, Nick Spitzer, John F. Szwed and Robert Farris Thompson. Blues for New Orleans: Mardi Gras and America's Creole Soul. Philadelphia: University of Pennsylvania Press, 2006). Diz was a master of mixing things together that often did not go together. He took risks others hesitated in taking. But he made you love him as he did so by turning his critique into a humorous comment or making it so seemingly outrageous that he couldn't really be serious. Except that, of course, he was. There was also a love for that which was human. At the height of the civil rights movement, I saw Dizzy drinking with a southern soldier who thought he was complimenting Diz, but was actually condescending to him. I sat at the bar expecting Diz to explode. Instead, he accepted the proffered drink, listened to the young soldier, and then made some off-handed remark that had the soldier laughing. The two walked off arm in arm. To me, this incident is illustrative of Dizzy's being able to occupy a number of cultures and identities simultaneously. He often understood exactly where others were coming from and found ways to be diplomatic while getting his point across. As with Armstrong, he found a way to live his life the way he wanted while also finding a way to criticize people in ways they first listened too because they were humorous. No surprise, then, that they were both superb jazz ambassadors, representing America, yes, but also the need for greater equality and democracy in America. They understood that while they had a dual heritage, that heritage was an overlapping one and could not be neatly segregated as others believed. They were this *and* that, too.

Ellington epitomized the blurring of categories in his music. It was hard to tell where one genre ended and another began. In so doing, he continued an African tradition and elevated his music to the realm of the sacred.

The Sacred

For Ellington, then, the sacred and spiritual appears to refer to that which promotes love and in the process provokes a sense of awe. Certainly, the quality of being life-affirming and inclusive is part of Ellington's conception of the sacred. Additionally, however, Ellington is aware of the power of ambiguity and humor in presenting his spiritual message. He is careful to allow dramatic pacing and juxtaposition of seeming opposites to tell his tale. As he stated, "A good playwright can say what he wants to say without saying it." It was a lesson he had learned early.

For example, the short 1929 movie Black and Tan Fantasy has a nice little story. The movie opens with Ellington and Artie Whetsol, one of his trumpet players, rehearsing. They need money and Fredi Washington, one of the Cotton Club dancers, informs Ellington and Whetsol that she is going back to work to help save Ellington's piano. Of course, Washington is in danger of dying, but performs anyway.

The movie features an authentic Cotton Club setting in which there is a brief but rather complete floorshow, featuring the famous Cotton Club Dancers. Fredi Washington dances, and then she collapses. After a spiritual, Black and Tan Fantasy is played. In sum, the movie is programmatic imitating a Cotton Club performance. This was a pattern that Ellington followed for much of his life.

What is often overlooked, however, is the manner in which Ellington dares to intersperse the sacred and the profane. There are not only echoes of spirituals or "church music" in his compositions. There are also outright spirituals used just before dancing that would offend many traditionally religious people. Moreover, that dancing takes place to a suite that has often been considered more religious in nature than secular. Ellington was blurring the distinction between two spheres that many other performers preferred to keep distinct, the sacred and the profane. By so doing he was placing his music in a category that he came to term "beyond category". He was also deeply involved in the realm that anthropologists recognize as that of the ambiguous and dangerous.

Steed (1993:3) notes this Ellington characteristic of avoiding categories. "Although he still personifies jazz for millions of people, Ellington did not even like to use the word unless it was defined simply as freedom of expression." Steed cites Dance (1970) who wrote:

> Duke Ellington never ceases to voice his disapproval of categories, which he views as a curb on an artist's right to freedom of expression. He always wants to be free to do what he feels moved to do, and not what someone feels he should do.

There is no doubt that Ellington felt that this mixing of categories had meaning beyond the music itself, that it was somehow sacred. He viewed his music as a vocation and as a means for breaking himself and other African Americans out of rigid categories, as his interview with Zunser (1930) makes absolutely clear. Ellington frequently explicitly noted his belief that music was a vocation, a sacred calling. At the Second Sacred Concert, for example, he labeled himself "God's messenger boy", a phrase repeated in the album notes (Steed 1993:6).

Steed (1993) includes this important passage from Stanley Dance's eulogy:

> Duke knew the good news was Love, of God and his fellow men. He proclaimed the message in his Sacred Concerts, grateful for an opportunity to acknowledge something of which he stood in awe, a power he considered above his human limitations.

For Ellington, attempts to capture that love and awe in his music, a love he viewed as transcending artificial differences and encompassing all life, were attempts at grasping the sacred. It is as if Ellington were saying that God has no limits. Limitations are human. Therefore, attempts to affirm life and love should also know no artificial limits.

Steed (1993:8) puts this issue in a slightly different, more musicological manner. At Ellington's funeral, a recording by Johnny Hodges of "Heaven" from the Second Sacred Concert was played. Steed notes the construction of the melody and some of its notable internal contrasts. One observation is relevant in ascertaining and understanding Ellington's conception of the sacred. "Ellington's favored tri-tone is heard three times, perversely ascending as if he were determined to make what was once called the 'devil's interval' angelic". This desire to force people to reconsider their stereotypical categorizations was a long-time project with Ellington that led logically to the Sacred Concerts.

This characteristic of blurring distinctions of asserting that what some think evil is a path to the good often irritated those who held traditional values. As Leonard (1962:21) notes, one of the major opponents of jazz included the guardians of traditional morality. Jazz violated the clear-cut values of this group through blurring indisputable distinctions and promoting ambiguity. Armstrong and Gillespie did so through their humor while Ellington subverted accepted reality through his embrace of the sacred, which differed from more traditional notions.

Discussion

In common with most western music, jazz structurally comprises melody, harmony, and rhythm. Somewhat simplistically, it has been common to assign its harmony to Europe, its rhythm to Africa, and to leave its melody somewhat up for grabs. Although there is some truth in this stereotype, it excludes rather more than it includes.

And jazz, in common with every other culture, has its own values, traditions, norms, history, and attitudes. It certainly has its own myths, both internal and external, as well; that is, myths its members generate to encapsulate and explain reality as well as myths outsiders have imposed upon it. Although both myths serve purposes, each type requires hermeneutical explication in order to yield deeper, rather than mere surface meanings.

Jazz, itself grew up out of the myth of Africa prevailing at the turn of the last century. Many authors have waxed eloquent on the ways in which "Africa" has been used to provide the western world with its images.

Hammond and Jablow (1977), for example, provide a useful introduction to the topic. Coetzee (1987:19) remarks:

> For centuries, in fact, it has been the fate of Africa to be employed by the west as a kind of image bank from which emblems—sometimes of savagery, brutality, and hopelessness, sometimes of innocence, simplicity and good nature—sometimes ... can be drawn at will. Mudimbe presents the best and most sophisticated treatment of this theme, the western invention of Africa. His calm philosophical treatment exposes the process through which "Africa" came to be invented and the consequences for Africa and the West of its invention.

Whatever the "prehistory" of jazz may have been, jazz itself begins with the consequences of the imposition of Jim Crow laws in New Orleans and the subsequent cultural clash between black Creoles and other blacks in New Orleans. Until the application of these laws, late in the nineteenth century, white and black musicians routinely performed together.

In 1903, W.E.B. Dubois articulated a theme that inheres in the very essence of African-American culture, namely, "the dual heritage of the black man in America". That heritage, African and European, is at root one of dual identity and a cause of a recurring crisis of identity, as DuBois went on to note. In a very real sense, the history of jazz has provided a dynamic model of the ever-changing terms of that heritage as well as a running commentary on it. It has done so through the use of tropes of identity.

Tropes encapsulate a culture's essence. Whatever a culture may be, however it views itself, it expresses that self-perception in select images packed with powerful meanings. Jazz is no exception. It, too, has its own cultural modes of expression, its personal symbols and metaphors that encapsulate and convey identity. Moreover, the best of these tropes are flexible and allow for the expression of changing concepts of self-identity.

"Africa" has been precisely that type of vehicle within jazz. It has served as a touchstone for gauging the state of the art as well as the self-image of its performers. Throughout jazz history, the concept of "Africa" has served as an index of authenticity. The less "African" and more "European" a performance, for example, the less likely jazz musicians are to find it acceptable. Conversely, the more authentic, even flawed, a performance, the more it is perceived to be approaching an African essence, or "soul"! Jazz musicians have been careful and correct in indicating that their music is not a result of inability or corruption in performance, but, rather, of choice. Two musical cultures consisting of related, but differing codes have been captured in the contrastive metaphors "African" and "European". These terms have not, of course, remained static over time.

Tracing the manner in which these contrastive terms have changed in meaning in the course of jazz's history provides an intriguing insight into both the genesis and change of jazz style and its cultural relationship to the increasing consciousness of its performers. Insight into that dialectical relationship, moreover, promises to lead to increasing understanding of the manner in which artists reinterpret cultural vehicles in order to convey their own personal visions of reality to fellow community members.

Thus, black musicians worked at perfecting styles that were uniquely their own. No other band could imitate the swing of the Basie band. No other band could be mistaken for Ellington's. His sophisticated use of harmonies and tone colors, inspired by French impressionistic music and painting, was unique In Jazz. Black soloists rarely had equals among white musicians. There were, of course, white musicians who were indeed originals, like Bunny Berrigan or Bix Beiderbecke. Significantly, these artists found themselves imitating their own African myth, one stressing outrageous living, unreliability and self-centeredness as prerequisites for creativity. It was but one more version of the myth of the "Noble Savage", documented by Hammond and Jablow (1977). It is an open question of just how much Euro-American art has been created through a misunderstanding of African art.

Throughout the post-war era, Africa's aura grew among jazz musicians. Certainly, the independence movement added to Africa's mystique and the linkage of Black Liberation with it was but natural. Islam became common among musicians long before it spread to other segments of the African American community. Armstrong's trip to Ghana was merely the most noticeable of many trips by jazz musicians to the continent. Africa increasingly became a metaphor of authenticity, of true identity within the black musical community and a trope of opposition to white exploitation of African Americans.

Certainly, images of Africa have long been part of jazz history. As I have argued, the contrast between "Africa" and "Europe" has provided dialectic of development for jazz itself. African elements have always formed part of the musical composition of jazz, and "jungle" images, for better or worse, have been used, willingly or not, by Ellington, Armstrong, and others. Many musicians have become Muslims in a belief that Islam is a more authentic African religion than Christianity and, thus, more appropriate for an African American.

In the 1960s, however, Black Nationalism became more openly dominant in jazz than it had ever been before in conformity with the self-conscious assertion of the right of blacks to control their own destiny, including their own identity. As America in general entered the confrontational politics of the late sixties, themes of identity—youth, gays, women, American Indians and blacks—became more pronounced. Initially, these assertions of identity tended to be separatist and exclusionary. The movement illustrated a very interesting contrast between black and white images of Africa in jazz. White musicians choose to be part of black culture. They are, however, free to move in and out of it at will. They are, therefore, always on trial by Black musicians and are aware of their probationary status. They tend to be both more romantic and fanatic about the mystique of Africa than most Black musicians who are more likely to use the concept as a tool—even as a weapon—in order to obtain their objectives.

There were a number of manifestations of the movement to Africanize jazz, but all of them shared the adjective "free". In some way, jazz was to be made "free". Indeed, even before the Black Power movement itself had jelled, Ornette Coleman had come on the scene in 1959 and, after an initial burst of enthusiasm, met with outright hostility. Within a few short years, however, many of his basic ideas were being followed.

In one very real and important sense jazz itself is the message. Its own meaning, to its practitioners and fans, changes over time as its social location alters and as the meaning of its "African/European" opposition varies. However, the situation is further complicated because each jazz musician and performance is meant to be creative, to generate meaning. Over and over, in one form or other, the principle is laid down that each musician must tell a story. Moreover, that story must be personal; one must live the story the music tells. In a truly essential way the medium is the message. Technique, for example, the ability to run chord changes accurately, to play fast or slow and still swing, is admired, but only a naïve listener admires it for its own sake. It must be used in the service of conveying a story. Charlie Parker, for example, is said to have advised aspiring saxophone players first to learn everything about their horns and then to forget it all when playing. Technique, in other words, is only a tool in allowing one's true inner self to be expressed. It is not admirable in and of itself. A knowledgeable insider sums up the position well when speaking about the early days of the bop revolution: "I never heard anyone play as fast as Bird. But it wasn't just speed. He had ideas no one else had" (Bob Redcross, personal communication).

Endeavoring to understanding the meaning of jazz, therefore, involves one in a series of exercises requiring the examination of multiple referents and cross-referents, of matching individual biographies to broader movements, specific variations to broader themes, and the ever-retreating just out of reach essence of the metaphor that is jazz itself, for to understand jazz is to understand the tertium quid that it is, namely, a symbol and encapsulation of America itself.

Conclusion

Ellington's love for things that are "beyond category" resonates with Levi-Strauss's categorization of anomalous mediating categories as dangerous and sacred (Levi-Strauss 1967, for example). These anomalous categories, according to Levi-Strauss, partake of the categories which they mediate and consequently are neither fish nor fowl. They are dangerous and somehow pollute. Mary Douglas (1966) has treated of these categories of pollution, an idea Neil Leonard (1987) has applied to jazz itself.

Leonard (1987-9-10) notes that Emile Durkheim, who influenced Douglas, indicated not only that there is a distinction between the sacred and the profane but between two kinds of sacredness. There is sacredness

> that produces social and moral order, health, and happiness ... There is also, however, an opposite sacred force that brings disorder, immorality, illness, and death. Though radically antagonistic, these two kinds of sacredness can be highly ambiguous because both stem from similar supernatural sources.

Interestingly, however, these types of sacredness appear to be highly unstable and each can resolve into the other. The musical "purist" seeks to keep them separate. Even in the African-American tradition there was a desire to keep the two traditions separate, as some opposition to Ellington's sacred concerts revealed.

There is, however, an older African tradition that understood the unity of the sacred. The variations work together to provide a harmonious whole. Each part both stands alone and yet takes on full meaning only within the context of the entire performance. This perspective is well-illustrated in the work of the Nigerian musician, Fela Anakulapi-Kuti.

In a sense, in his performance the Nigerian artist Fela added to Gregory Bateson's and Erving Goffman's concept of frames, turning frames into shifting things, ones that almost perpetually transform themselves into one another. This house-of-mirror image of shifting frames is in keeping with the predominant perspective on African religious and philosophical thought that sees it as positing an ever-changing unstable reality under the illusory permanent reality of every-day common sense. This skepticism of the presented reality and a subsequent search for underlying structures is well-suited to African-derived musical performance.

Therefore, the incorporation of all varieties of African-derived music is not accidental or haphazard. It serves to convey his message of Black Pride. His point is the unity of black peoples everywhere. The manner in which he conveys his message displays the technical brilliance that is appreciated when it is suited to the message. Thus, his shifting frames reflect African religion and philosophy. The manner in which one style of African-derived music melds into another defines their relationship through praxis not mere discussion. The central role of jazz, a word Fela disdained as did Ellington, is demonstrated in its being used as a mediating form.

Finally, the continuous transformation of material is also evocative of spiritual matters. Fittingly, the self-proclaimed Black President and Chief Priest led his people to a better land through invoking spiritual images and enacting them on the stage. His entire performance is ritual of a high order. It is a Creole performance that has the "that too" characteristic of all such performances (James Farris Thompson, personal communication). Thus, there was no contradiction in Fela's performance. Each element was an integral part of the overriding message and enabled the performance to move toward an end he deemed sacred, the true emancipation of the Black man and the instilling of pride in his mind.

What is true of Fela illuminates Ellington's mixture of styles and categories. It would be beneficial to explore Ellington's African roots more deeply and to investigate his own reading in greater detail in relationship to his music (Hudson 1991). It is clear that Ellington's religion struck orthodox Christians as pantheistic and idiosyncratic (Steed 1993:pp. 19ff. and Gensel 1992). His statement that he was "born in 1956 at the Newport Jazz Festival Hasse" (1993:322) was often cited but never fully explored. The religious connotations are often noted, but the literal sense in which Ellington meant the term has been missed. He believed that somehow he had been literally reborn and called to a vocation.

Seen within the context of African American culture Ellington's religious beliefs and practices make perfect sense, even those "superstitious" aspects which so bothered his more traditionally orthodox son Mercer (Mercer Ellington and Dance 1978:111). The continuity between the Cotton Club and the Cathedral is emphasized by Ellington's very African American philosophy and theology. His mixture of categories of the sacred and profane and various types of sacredness is an affirmation of both life and the continuous nature of that life, transcending stereotypical traditional categories.

Jazz culture, then, challenges mainstream culture in a number of ways. Through indirect and direct subversion—humor and confrontation—it asserts a reality contrasting with accepted presupposed cultural reality. The presuppositions of the accepted worldview are generally held up to questioning, upsetting true believers. Thus, whether the sacred clown, the genial sophisticated religious performer, or the angry confrontationalist challenges accepted reality through performance, jazz can disturbingly challenge one's notions of cultural reality and often does. It subverts accepted reality through offering its own perspective, sometimes comic and sometimes angry, of what reality could be, prompting listeners to think of just might be a better world.

Coda

The trickster crosses boundaries and creates a new reality, one most people never imagine. With just a handful of notes in a scale they weave new vistas, adding to the work of those great musicians who came before them, often finding hidden beauty in what once was deemed ugly. Like Trickster, they improvise on the spot, erecting musical structures on existing forms. People like Sonny Rollins or his idol, Charlie Parker, create on the spot expanding the music. Like Trickster they see those who mocked them imitate them, copying their innovations until they become clichés.

Like Trickster, the great musicians never lose their ability to surprise. I have listened to the greats every day of my life, and am every day surprised by their work. Enrico Rava, the Italian avant-garde trumpet player, told me that he wakes up and listens to Louis Armstrong, stating that he always finds something new he can use in his own playing. The true trickster is always one step ahead of the rest of us. In music, we are always striving to catch up with the great creative geniuses.

Trickster in mythology is often either a god or a demi-god. He is an opponent of the established order; for some he, or she, is a hero. For others, however, he is a dangerous villain, one who disturbs the balance of life. One does not have to spend much time among jazz musicians to see how creative their language is and to note the depth of their perceptions. My wife once accompanied to a jazz club where we sat with the trio members during the break. When we left, she stated that she, a rock fan, could find that high level of discussion among rock musicians.

Allowing for some important exceptions, she is correct. The men and women are always full of surprises. Ella Fitzgerald, for example, forgetting her lyrics to "Mack the Knife" in a live performance improvised lyrics on the spot. She could have simply scatted over the chords. She chose to keep going, adding the spice of humor and humility to the performance. Sara Vaughan, creating a new melody over a song's chords while retaining the original lyrics, not only kept those fans that never or rarely listen to instrumentals, but also educated them at the same time.

The marvelous Stan Getz, who never composed a song on paper, never failed to compose new melodies each time he put his tenor sax to his lips. And what can one say of Miles Davis, whom Dizzy Gillespie termed the Prince of Darkness? He was a man always reinventing himself, even when he strayed from the beautiful tone and the superb note choice that marked his greatest musical success. Ironically, when asked why he did not forget the pop-funk and electronic abstractions of his later period, he said that if he tried to play straight-ahead lyric music, he would give himself a heart attack. Like the Trickster he was, he predicted his death. He did return to playing gorgeous music and he died soon after—of a heart attack. He gave us a sad surprise.

Surprise is synonymous with Trickster. It keeps us mere mortals alive. It keeps us on our toes and lets us vicariously feel the thrill of living on the edge, like Charles Mingus's Clown on his tightrope. The zigs and zags of Trickster's progress through life captivate us. Trickster's appetites for life often get him, or her, in trouble. But just as often they lead to something marvelous—like authentic jazz!

BIBLIOGRAPHY

"Charlie Parker, Jazz Master, Dies." 16 March:1. 1955

"Lee Morgan!" 20 Feb.:34. 1972

Blues for New Orleans: Mardi Gras and America's Creole Soul. Philadelphia: University of Pennsylvania Press. 2006

Abrahams; Roger.. The Man-of-Words in the West Indies. Baltimore: Johns Hopkins University Press. 1983

Ake, David. Jazz Cultures. Berkeley: University of California Press, 2002.

Ammons, Elizabeth and Annette White-Pak (eds.) Tricksterism in Turn-of-the-Century American Literature: A Multicultural Perspective. Hanover, NH: University Press of New England. 1994

Armstrong, Louis, Thomas Brothers (Editor) Louis Armstrong, in His Own Words: Selected Writings. New York: Oxford University Press, 2001.

Balliett, Whitney. "The Measure of Bird." Saturday Review 17 March 1956:33-34.

Bateson, Gregory. A theory of play and fantasy. In Bateson, G. (ed.), Steps to an Ecology of Mind. San Francisco: Chandler, 173-193. . 1972

Becker, Howard S. *Outsiders:* Studies in the Sociology of Deviance. New York: Free Press. 1963

Bergreen, Laurence Louis Armstrong: An Extravagant Life. New York: Broadway Books. 1995

Boskin, Joseph Sambo: The Rise and Decline of the American Jester. New York: Oxford.1986

—.Rebellious Laughter: People's Humor in American Culture. Syracuse: 1997

Boskin, Joseph and Joseph Dorinson. Ethnic Humor: Subversion and Survival. American Quarterly 37, 81–971983; also In Walker, Nancy A. (ed.), What's So Funny: Humor in American Culture. Wilmington, DE: Scholarly Resources, 205–224. 1998

Baldwin, James "Many Thousands Gone." Notes of a Native Son. 1955. Boston: Beacon,. 24-45. 1984

Boulard, Garr. Blacks, Italians, and the Making of New Orleans Jazz. The Journal of Ethnic Studies 16:1:53-66, 1995

Boulard, Garry. Louis Prima (Music in American Life).University of Illinois Press, 2002 (first published in 1989)

Burma, J. H. Humor as a Technique in Race Conflict. American Sociological Review 11, 710–715. 1946

Cameron, William Bruce. "Sociological Notes on the Jam Session." *Social Forces*, 33(2):177-82. 1954

Collier, James L. Louis Armstrong: an American Genius. New York: Oxford University Press. 1983

Charlie Parker – Koko http://lcweb4.loc.gov/natlib/ihas/service/mulligan/100010952/0001.pdf 1995.

—. Cherokee. http://www.youtube.com/watch?v=okrNwE6GI70&feature=related

Cox, Harvey *he Feast of Fools: A theological essay on festivity and fantasy* Cambridge Mass: Harvard University Press .1969

Dance, Stanley. Album Notes to MCAAC "Duke Ellington's Orchestral Works" with Erich Dickson.1970

Davis, Miles. *Miles: The Autobiography.* Simon & Schuster; 1rst Preston Edition. 1990

Desmond, Paul. Paul Desmond interviews Charlie Parker. This is a radio broadcast from early 1954 (probably March) in Boston, Mass. with announcer John McLellan. 1954

Dickson-Carr, Darryl. African American Satire: The Sacredly Profane Novel: University of Missouri Press, 2001

Douglas, Mary Purity and Danger: An Analysis of the Concepts of Pollution and Tabo. 1984

Du Bois, W. E. B.The Souls of Black Folks. Chicago: A.C. McClurg & CO.1903

Ford, Iris Carter. The Travel and Travail of Negro Showpeople. Anthropology & Humanism 26, No. 1:35-45. 2006

Ellington, Edward Kennedy. The Duke Steps Out. Rhythm March: 20-22. 1931

—.Music Is My Mistress. New York: Da Capo. Orig. 1973.

Ellington, Mercer with Stanley Dance.. Duke Ellington in Person: An Intimate Memoir. Boston: Houghton Mifflin. 1978

Ellison, Ralph. Invisible Man. New York: Random House.. 1952

Erasmus, Desiderius. *The Praise of Folly.* 1511. Trans. Hoyt Hopewell Hudson. Princeton, NJ: Princeton UP, 1941.

Feather, Leonard: A Bird's-ear View of Music. Nobody gets the bird from bird as broadminded parker takes the blindfold test, in: Metronome, 64/8 (Aug.), p. 14. 21-22 1948

Giddins, Gary. Celebrating Bird. The Triumph of Charlie Parker. New York: Beech Tree. 1987

Gillespie, D. with Fraser, A. To Be or Not to Bop: Memoirs of Dizzy Gillespie. New York: Da Capo Press.1979

Gofffman, Erving. Stigma: Notes on the Management of Spoiled Identity. New York: Simon &Schuster. 1963

—.. Frame Analysis: An Essay on the Organization of Experience. Boston: Northeastern University Press. [1974] 1986

Guida, George. Las Vegas Jubilee: Louis Prima's 1950s Stage Act as Multicultural Pageant The Journal of Popular Culture 38:e 678 678-697,2005.

Hasse, John Edward. Beyond Category: The Life and Genius of Duke Ellington. NY: Simon & Schuster. 1993

Hentoff, Nat. "Wynton Is Right." Jazz Times 7.1989

Huizinga, Johan. Homo Ludens: A Study of the Play-Element in Culture. Beacon, 1955.

Hyde, Lewis Herndon, M and N. McLeod Trickster Makes This World: Mischief, Myth and Art. New York: Farrar, Straus, Giroux. 1998

Hynes, W. J. 'Inconclusive Conclusions: Tricksters: Metaplayers and Revellers' in Hynes, W. J. and Doty, W. G. Mythical Trickster Figures, Tuscaloosa & London: University of Alabama Press, 202-19. 1993

Joe Venuti/Tony Romano Never Before...Never Again. Just a Memory Records - JAM-9127-2. 2000.

Jones, Leroi .Blues People. New York: William Morrow. 1967

Jung, Carl "On the Psychology of the Trickster Figure." Collected Works Trans. R.F.C. Hull. Radin 195-211.1954-1966

Kempton, Murray. "Flown Bird." *New York Post.* 22 March 1955.

Lamont, Michele and Marcel Fournier, eds.Cultivating Differences: Symbolic Boundaries and the making of Inequality. Chicago, IL: University of Chicago Press. 1992

Leonard, Neil. Jazz—Myth and Religion. Oxford University Press, 1987.

Levi-Strauss, Claude. The structural study of myth. American Folklore 68, 426-444. 1955

Lock Helen, 'Transformations of the Trickster 18 Southern Cross Review, 2002

Lyotard, J-F. La Condition Postmoderne, Paris: Minuit. 1979

Mingus, Charles. The Clown. New York: Atlantic Record Corporation.. 1961 (1984).

Mudimbe, V. Y. The Invention of Africa. Bloomington: Indiana University Press. 1988

Mulligan, Gerry.

Autobiography.http://www.loc.gov/item/ihas.100010952
New York Amsterdam News. "Diz at Birdland." 19 March: 8 1955
New York Magazine. "Bird!' 7 March; 7. 1983
New York News World. "If you don't Live *It*, It Won't Come Out of Your Horn: Charlie Parker, Iwo-1955." 10 Nov. 1979
New York Post, "Jazz World Mourns Loss of 'Cool' Charlie Parker." /6 March 1966: i. "Parker Tribute: Fiasco at Fisher." 26 Aug. 1975:24.
New York Worker. "Charlie Parker Memorial jams Carnegie Hall." 4 April 1951
Panassie, Hughes. Louis Armstrong. New York: Scribner's, 1971.
Parker, Chan, with Francis Poitiers Paudras. Bird with Love. Paris: Wizlov, 1981.
Pelton, Robert D. The Trickster in West Africa. Berkeley: University of California Press. 1980
Pratt Ray Praeger, Rhythm and Resistance: Explorations in the Political Uses of Popular Music New York: Praeger. 1990
Radin, Paul. The Trickster. Philosophical Library. 1956
Reisner, Robert. *Bird: The Legend of Charlie Parker*. New York: Citadel P, 1962.
—. *Bird: The Legend of Charlie Parker*. New York: Citadel P, 1962.
Riesman, David, Nathan Glazer and Reuel Denney. The Lonely Crowd. New Haven, CT: Yale University Press. [1950] 2001
Rodney, Red. "Interview" On Charlie Parker, One Night in Washington (album). n.d.
Salamone, F.A. "Leaping Before Looking: An Analysis of the Attica Relations.1977
Salamone, Frank A. "Epistemological Implications of Fieldwork and Their Consequences." American Anthropologist, 81:146-160. 1979
—. "The Force Primeval: An Image of Jazz in American Literature." Play & Culture. 3(3):256-266, 1990.
—. "Laughin' Louie: An Analysis of Louis Armstrong's Record and its Relationship to African-American Musical Humor." Humor: International Journal of Humor Research 15.1 47-64. 2002
—. "George Shearing: Interview." Cadence. 16(4):5-8, 24. 1990
—.. Religions as play: Bori, a friendly witchdoctor. Journal of Religion in Africa 8:201-211. 1976
—.Close Enough for Jazz: The Nature of Jazz Humor. Humor. 1:371-388. 1988 a
—.The ritual of jazz performance. Play and Culture 1:85-104. 1988b
—. Bringin' It All Back Home! Studies in Third World Societies 46:53-63. 1991

Salamone, Frank. Interview with Gap Mangione. Cadence June: 11-14, 1990.

Salazar, Man. "Interview with Machito (Frank Grillo)" Files of the Institute of Jazz Studies, 1980.

Sidran Ben Black Talk New York: DaCapo Press.1998

Smith, Jeanne Rosier. Writing Tricksters: Mythic Gambols in American Ethnic Literature. Berkeley, CA: University of California Press. 1994

Steed, Janna. Duke Ellington: A Spiritual Biography (Lives & Legacies). New York: The Crossroads Publishing Company. 1999

Storey, John.. "Rockin'Hegemony: West Coast Rock and Amerika's War in Vietnam." Pp. 88-97 in Cultural Theory and Popular Culture, edited by John Storey. Harlow, UK: Pearson Education Ltd. 2009

Sullivan, Jack. New World Symphonies. New Haven: Yale University Press, 1999

The Church of St. John Coltrane. African Orthodox Church. Accessed February 12,.http://www.coltranechurch.org/. 2013

Thompson, Robert Farris. 1985 Flash of the Spirit: African and Afro-American Art and Philosophy. New York: Vintage.

TVTropeshttp://tvtropes.org/pmwiki/pmwiki.php/Main/TheTrickster?from=Main.Tricksters first Accessed May 5, 2012

Ugorji, Okechukwu K. The Adventures of Torti: Tales from West Africa. Trenton, NJ: African World Press, 1991.

Vizenor, Gerald. The Trickster of Liberty. Minneapolis: U of Minneapolis.1988.

—. Darkness in Saint Louis Bearheart. St. Paul: Truck P, 1978. Rpt. as Bearheart: The Heirship Chronicles. Minneapolis: U of Minnesota P, 1990.

—. Griever: An American Monkey King in China. Minneapolis: U of Minnesota P, 1987.

West, Candace and Don H. Zimmerman. *Gender & Society*, 1(2):125-151. 1987

Welsford, Enid. The Fool: His Social and Literary History. 1935. Gloucester, MA: Peter Smith, 1966

Whitman, Walt. Whitman's *Song of Myself.* http://www.english.illinois.edu/maps/poets/s_z/whitman/song.htm first Accessed October 25, 2012

Wyatt, Hugh. "Tribute of Charlie Parker" *New York News* 24 April:34. Williams, 1983

Zwerin, Michael.Close Enough for Jazz. New York: Quartet. 1983

Interviews

Anakulapi-Kuti, Fela. Personal Interview. Lagos, Nigeria. 1989
Ryerson, Ali. Personal interview. White Plains, NY.1985.
Dance, Stanley and Helen Dance. Interview with Jay McShann. December 11, 1978. Transcript at Institute of Jazz Studies. Rutgers University, Newark. 1978
Ross, Mattie.. Personal interviews. London, England.1985 and 1986

INDEX

aesthetics, 46
African, iii, v, 6, 8, 10, 11, 13, 14, 16, 17, 18, 20, 21, 22, 23, 24, 25, 27, 29, 31, 32, 33, 34, 35, 36, 42, 45, 47, 49, 50, 51, 52, 54, 55, 56, 57, 58, 59, 60, 61, 62, 63, 67, 69, 70, 71, 72, 73, 75, 76, 77, 79, 80, 81, 82, 83, 89, 90
African art., 54
African-American, v, 6, 8, 14, 16, 21, 22, 24, 27, 89
Africa's, 58, 80
arbitrariness, iv, v
archetype, iii, 23
Armstrong, 2, 6, 7, 8, 9, 16, 19, 20, 21, 22, 23, 24, 27, 29, 37, 38, 41, 55, 56, 57, 58, 66, 67, 68, 70, 74, 75, 78, 80
authority, iv
Bateson, 82
be-bop, 6
Bird, iv, 2, 3, 4, 6, 7, 9, 10, 11, 12, 13, 87
Bird., 64, 81
Birdland, 43, 70
Black, 37, 41, 42, 47, 50, 52, 53, 54, 55, 56, 57, 58, 59, 60, 61, 62, 65, 67, 70, 76, 79, 80, 81, 82, 83
Black and Tan Fantasy, 76
Black music, 6, 16
boundaries, iii, iv, v, 6, 8, 11, 25, 26, 28, 84
Charles Mingus, 46
Charlie Parker, 1, iii, iv, v, 1, 4, 6, 9, 11, 12, 13, 15, 17, 29, 63, 68, 70, 81, 84, 86
clown, 4, 15, 16, 17
conformity, iv
Cotton Club, 76, 83

Creole, 20, 28, 37, 50, 53, 62, 67, 73, 75, 83
culture, iii, iv, 6, 7, 8, 16, 23, 24, 27
Culture, 36, 65, 67
cultures, iii, v, 21, 28
Diz, 68, 69, 70, 71, 72, 75
Diz,, 3
Dizzy, 38, 44, 47, 49, 58, 68, 70, 71, 72, 75
Dizzy Gillespie, iv, 1, 6, 7, 9, 11, 12, 15, 19, 38, 44, 47, 49, 58, 68, 70, 72, 84
Du Bois, 73
Durkheim, 82
Ella Fitzgerald, 19, 84
Ellington, 1, 29, 47, 56, 57, 59, 69, 76, 77, 78, 80, 81, 82, 83
Eshu, 74
European, 35, 38, 49, 50, 52, 53, 57, 60, 62, 63, 79, 81
Fela, 1, 2, 17, 22, 70, 82, 83
fool, 2, 25, 26
Gerry Mulligan, 9
Goffman, 82
Hawkins, 58
humor, iv, 2, 7, 15, 17, 18, 19, 20, 21, 22, 27, 84
Humor, 67, 70, 71
humor., iv, 2, 17, 21, 23
improvisation, iv, 11, 24
Infants of the Spring, 72
interactions, iii
interviews, 61
Italian Americans, 36, 38, 45
Jack Teagarden's, 67
James Baldwin wrote, 73
jazz, iv, v, 1, 2, 4, 6, 7, 8, 9, 10, 11, 12, 15, 17, 18, 19, 20, 23, 25, 27, 28, 29, 35, 36, 37, 38, 39, 40, 41, 43, 44, 45, 46, 47, 48,

49, 50, 51, 52, 53, 54, 55, 56, 57, 58, 59, 60, 61, 62, 63, 64, 65, 66, 68, 69, 70, 71, 72, 73, 74, 77, 78, 79, 80, 81, 82, 83, 84, 85
JAZZ, 2, iii, iv, v, 1, 5, 6, 7, 10, 12, 14, 15, 16, 27, 28, 29, 32, 34, 35, 36, 37, 38, 39, 43, 44, 45, 47, 49, 50, 51, 52, 65, 72, 73, 74, 76, 78, 79, 80, 83
John Coltrane, 60, 61, 65
Keil, 68
Leonard, 65, 73, 78, 82
Levi-Strauss, 62, 81
Little Jazz, 73
Louis Armstrong, iv, 1, 2, 4, 5, 6, 7, 9, 11, 12, 14, 16, 19, 23, 27, 36, 37, 38, 41, 66, 68, 70, 72, 74, 75, 84, 89
mediating, 25, 26
metaphor, 58, 64, 74, 80, 81
Mozart, 56
music, 35, 37, 38, 41, 42, 43, 44, 46, 47, 48, 49, 50, 51, 52, 53, 55, 56, 57, 58, 59, 60, 61, 62, 63, 65, 66, 68, 70, 71, 72, 73, 74, 75, 76, 77, 78, 79, 80, 81, 82, 83
Music, 36, 37, 43, 60
musicians, 35, 36, 37, 38, 39, 40, 41, 43, 44, 45, 46, 47, 49, 50, 53, 54, 56, 57, 58, 59, 61, 62, 65, 66, 68, 70, 73, 79, 80
mythology, 5, 16, 84
New Orleans, 1, 9, 11, 20, 24, 28
Nigeria, 69, 74

Parker, iv, 1, 2, 5, 6, 8, 9, 10, 16
Paul Radin's, 5
performance, 39, 42, 43, 44, 49, 52, 54, 58, 62, 63, 65, 71, 73, 76, 79, 81, 82, 83
Pete, 39
religion, 1, 5, 16, 23, 29
ritual, 83
Robert Farris Thompson, 75
ROCHESTER, 35, 42, 43, 44, 45, 70
Sacred, 76, 77
Satchmo, 2, 3, 11, 20, 21, 41, 66, 69, 72
saxophone, 44, 60, 63, 81
spirituality, 1, 2, 18
subcultures, iii, v
subversive humor, iv
Swing, 55, 56, 57, 71
tenor sax, 71
transcendent, 1
transcending, iii, 28
transformative, 29
trickster, iii, iv, v, 7, 11, 12, 15, 16, 25, 26, 27, 69, 70, 74, 75
Trickster, 1, iii, 2, 5, 6, 8, 10, 11, 12, 13, 14, 15, 16, 17, 21, 23, 24, 25, 26, 27, 28, 29, 30, 31, 32, 33, 66, 68, 69, 70, 75, 84, 85, 87, 88, 90
tricksters, iii, iv, v, 6, 10, 16
Tropes, 49, 79
truth to power, 2, 17
Vipers, 66, 75
West Africa, 35, 67
Yoruba, 2, 17, 18, 23, 27, 30